Dear Bronx Zoo

Joyce Altman & Sue Goldberg

Foreword by Douglas Falk, Assistant Curator,
Education Department, Bronx Zoo

Macmillan Publishing Company   New York

Collier Macmillan Canada   Toronto

Maxwell Macmillan International Publishing Group
New York   Oxford   Singapore   Sydney

ACKNOWLEDGMENTS

Our special thanks to the following people at the Bronx Zoo without whose help and support this book would not have been possible: Dr. William Conway, John McKew, Annette Berkovits, Douglas Falk, Carole Ferster, Sheila Goldberg, Adriane Maisell, Bill Meng, Dennis DeMello, Kathy Boldt, "Sunday A" Friends of the Zoo, and all of the staff members who generously gave of their knowledge and expertise.

We are also grateful to those whose guidance and encouragement has proven invaluable: Billy Altman, Jon and Jennie Goldberg, Marion and Hal Persons, Judy and Paul Hoppe, Barbara Bader, and our editor, Judith Whipple.

Macmillan Publishing Company
866 Third Avenue, New York, NY 10022
Collier Macmillan Canada, Inc.
1200 Eglinton Avenue East
Suite 200
Don Mills, Ontario M3C 3N1
First Edition
Printed in the United States of America

10 9 8 7 6 5 4 3 2 1
The text of this book is set in 13 point ITC Garamond Light.

Library of Congress Cataloging-in-Publication Data
Altman, Joyce.
Dear Bronx Zoo/by Joyce Altman and Sue Goldberg;
foreword by Douglas Falk.—1st ed.   p.   cm.
Includes bibliographical references (p.   ).
Summary: Describes the activities at the Bronx Zoo and
introduces the animals on display.
ISBN 0-02-700640-9
1. New York Zoological Park—Juvenile literature.
2. Zoo animals—Juvenile literature. [1. New York Zoological Park.
2. Zoos. 3. Zoo animals.] I. Goldberg, Sue. II. Title.
QL76.5.U62N4814   1990   590'.74'4747275—dc20   89-28226   CIP   AC

Contents

For my father, Arnold Moskowitz, who taught me through his example to love and respect all living things —J. A.·

To Jon and Jennie for all their invaluable help, and for their love and friendship —S. G.

Foreword

A young child once asked in a letter to the Bronx Zoo: "What new plans are in the future for the zoo?" This child anticipated that changes would reshape the zoo. He was right. Wilderness is vanishing as humans develop the planet. The wildlife that we once knew is being reduced to survival in little isolated pockets of nature surrounded by people and their activities. Today's children, more than ever before, have little or no opportunity for firsthand contact with wildlife in nature. Where will children have this experience? For most, it will be at the zoo. The zoo is where children see their storybook animals come to life. The Bronx Zoo strives to depict nature's landscapes ever more realistically and teach children what wild animals need for survival. And in the zoo, where the animals aren't mere images on a page or screen, the impact of wildlife causes questions to burst forth from young minds. These questions, which are addressed in this book, tell us of the wonder that children feel when they observe wild animals. Just as the zoo itself is a celebration of life, this book celebrates the marvelous curiosity of children about life.

Douglas Falk
Assistant Curator
Education Department,
Bronx Zoo

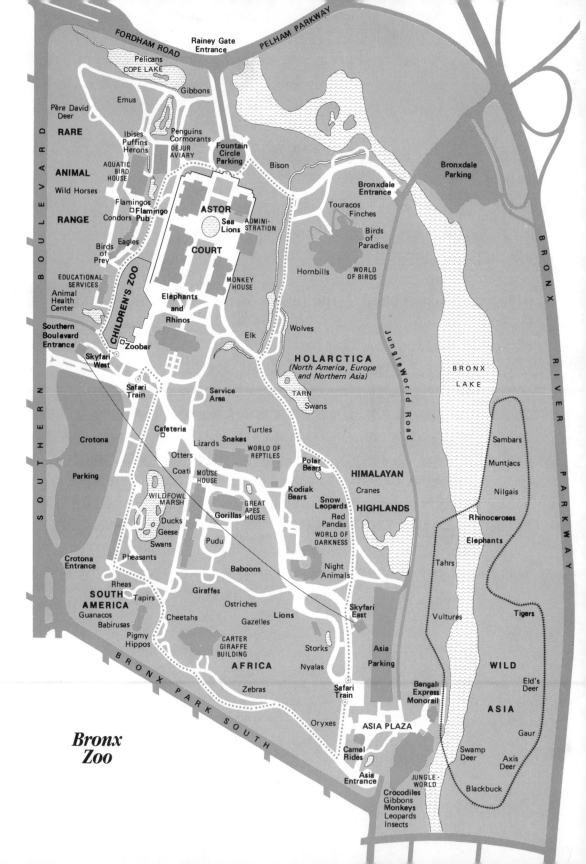

Bronx Zoo

Introduction

Every day, letters arrive at the Bronx Zoo. Most come from children—children who've recently come to the zoo, or who live too far away to visit. When they write, they ask about all aspects of animal and zoo life, everything from "Do bats always hang upside down?" and "Why does the rattlesnake have a rattle?" to "Where do the animals sleep at night when it's cold?"

The letters are answered by the Friends of the Zoo, a group of volunteers who work with the zoo's education department to teach and inform zoo visitors about animals. In answering these letters, as well as the questions posed at the zoo by young zoo visitors, Sue Goldberg and I, both members of the Friends of the Zoo, conceived the idea for *Dear Bronx Zoo*—a collection of the best and most frequently asked zoo-related questions. The answers explain how animals live in nature and captivity, how the zoo operates and cares for over 4,200 animals on a day-to-day basis, and what role modern-day zoos play in species preservation.

Accompanying the text are photos of zoo animals from the Bronx Zoo's photo library, and a 100-word glossary to help with the meanings of new vocabulary words.

Children are our future, and it will be their love and respect for nature and wildlife that will assure the survival of animal species. This book seeks to help children better understand the world around them as well as their important place within it.

Joyce Altman

Behind the Scenes

What is a zoo?

For many people, especially those who live in cities, the only way to ever see wild animals is by visiting a zoo. In the past, most zoos only displayed strange and unusual animals for people to look at, but today they do much more than that. Modern zoos not only exhibit animals, but also teach people about wildlife and the environment, and even help to preserve animals that are losing their homes in nature.

The Bronx Zoo exhibits animals from all parts of the world, sends researchers into the field to study animals in the wild, and working together with other zoos, helps preserve many **endangered species**—those animals that are in danger of dying out, or becoming **extinct.** As animals lose more and more of their natural ranges, called **habitats,** zoos help provide substitute homes for them.

More than 4,200 wild animals from all over the world live at the Bronx Zoo, a 265-acre zoological park in New York City.

In the past, zoos tried to display as many different types of animals as possible. Modern zoos, instead, keep fewer kinds of animals, or animal **species,** so that they can care for and **breed** larger numbers of each. By doing so, they give the animals a better chance of survival.

When did the Bronx Zoo open? How big is it?

The Bronx Zoo opened in 1899, four years after the New York Zoological Society was formed. Although not the oldest zoo in the United States (the Cincinnati and Philadelphia zoos are older), it is one of the country's largest and most successful urban zoos, with 265 acres of meadows and woodlands.

From the beginning, animal exhibition at the Bronx Zoo was different than at many other zoos of the day. Instead of small pens, the zoo housed many of its animals in open areas similar to their natural habitats. Large North American animals, such as deer, elk, and bison, ranged in large enclosed meadows, and the natural landscapes helped give zoo visitors a truer sense of the animals' nature and ways.

Today's exhibits are designed to resemble natural habitats even more closely. For example, one of the newer exhibits at the Bronx Zoo, the Himalayan Highlands, houses red pandas, rare white-naped cranes, tragopan pheasants, and a highly endangered species of cat called the snow leopard in large mountainous and marshy outdoor areas created especially for them. In the JungleWorld building, Asian mammals, birds, and reptiles of all descriptions live in huge, barless habitats, so real that it's easy to imagine what it's like in the Asian wilderness.

Where is the Bronx Zoo located? Who owns it?

The zoo is located in a borough of New York City called the Bronx, just north of Manhattan. The zoo is part of the New York Zoological Society. The society is a private, nonprofit organization which also operates the New York Aquarium and Osborn Laboratories of Marine Sciences in Brooklyn, New York; Wildlife Conservation International (WCI), a worldwide organization that participates in fieldwork, research, and **conservation** projects around the world; and the Wildlife Survival Center on St. Catherine's Island in the state of Georgia. At the Georgia center, the zoo is involved in **captive propagation** of endangered species and their return—when possible—to the wild.

The society also manages the recently rebuilt Central Park Zoo in New York City.

How many animals are in the Bronx Zoo? How many babies are born each year?

The zoo has over 4,200 resident animals of over 650 species and subspecies. More than 1,000 animals are born or hatched each year in the zoo.

Where does the Bronx Zoo get its animals from?

Because zoos today are concerned with protecting animal populations, they generally no longer seek animals captured in the wild for their collections. Also, it is very upsetting for any

Siberian tiger cubs are among the many endangered species that have been captive bred at the zoo in recent years.

animal to be taken from its home or family. Many captured animals do not survive. For some rare species, taking individuals from the wild may push the species closer to extinction.

Instead of collecting animals from the wild, pairs or groups of animals live together in zoos and produce babies. Animals that breed in zoos are called **captive bred.** Since not all zoos breed all species of animals, exchanges and loans are often made between zoos. Zookeepers keep records on their animals—such as the age, sex, and condition of each—so that loans (sometimes long term) can be made. These loans and exchanges are important when it comes to efforts to save endangered species. In order for a species that has lost a lot of its population to remain healthy and survive, its remaining members must breed and produce young with nonrelated members of the same species. Most zoos do not have the facilities to keep a large number of animals of each species, so exchanging animals from one zoo with those from another becomes essential.

In a single year, the Bronx Zoo may exchange as many as five hundred animals with over one hundred other institutions. When one of the zoo's animals is sent to another zoo for a temporary or long-term stay for breeding purposes, that animal is on "breeding loan."

How many people visit the Bronx Zoo each year?

Over 2 million people visit the zoo yearly. Among those visitors are about 350,000 students. The zoo is open 365 days a year, and charges admission on Fridays through Mondays; donations are accepted on the other days. Senior citizens and infants are always admitted free. Admission fees are used toward the upkeep of the zoo.

How much does it cost to feed and care for the animals?

Running the zoo costs over $22 million a year; the cost of running the entire New York Zoological Society and all of its programs is $40 million a year. The New York Zoological Society has over thirty thousand members who help support the zoo and aquarium through their membership dues. In addition, the zoo receives donations from individuals, foundations, and corporations.

Are most of the zoo's exhibits in buildings or outdoors?

There are combinations of indoor and outdoor exhibits at the zoo. Indoor exhibits include: the World of Birds, the Aquatic Bird House, the World of Darkness, the Reptile House, the Great Apes House, JungleWorld, the Giraffe Building, the Mouse House, the Monkey House, and the Elephant House. Outdoor ranges include: South America, Africa, Wild Asia, Holarctica, Bird Valley, and the Rare Animal Range. There is also a wildfowl marsh, a small mountain lake called a **tarn,** a lake and island where gibbons and pelicans live in the warm months, a flamingo pond, and a huge aviary for penguins and other water birds.

What is the most popular building at the zoo?

The Reptile House, the zoo's oldest building, is always filled with visitors who come to see the many species of snakes, turtles, crocodiles, frogs, toads, lizards, and other reptiles and amphibians on display. There are many rare and unusual creatures in this building. One is called the Lake Titicaca frog. It can remain submerged in water almost indefinitely, getting oxygen through its skin. When water comes into contact with the frog's loose folds of thin skin, the frog extracts the oxygen it needs from the water. Another is the Gila monster, a smallish (17- to 24-inch) lizard from the southwestern part of the United States, and one of only two poisonous lizards in the world. (The other is the Mexican beaded lizard.)

The Elephant House is another favorite building. It houses Asian elephants, Indian rhinoceroses, and Malayan tapirs.

Among the outdoor exhibits, the Children's Zoo is also quite popular. Here children can see animals at close range—prairie dogs and herons, raccoons and skunks, foxes and porcupines, ducks and goats, and many more. And they can learn how these animals use their senses, build homes, and defend themselves.

What do animals at the zoo eat, and how often are they fed?

Each animal in the zoo has its own special diet and eating schedule, which vary depending on what type of animal it is. The zoo's nutritionist works with the curators, keepers, and **veterinarians** (zoo doctors) to determine the exact foods necessary for the good health of each species. Sometimes a diet must be invented, such as proper baby food for an orphaned sea lion or for a litter of snow leopard cubs.

Some animals, like birds and tigers, may eat only once a day. Others, like sea lions, are fed twice daily. Snakes may eat only once a week.

Meat, chicken, and fish for the carnivores are usually bought in large quantities, then frozen and stored in a warehouse until needed. Polar bears sometimes enjoy being fed their fish still frozen in a block of ice, so they can play with it as it melts.

Some of the animals at the zoo eat very large quantities of food. Elephants are each fed about seventeen pounds of sweet grain daily, along with as much hay as they want (usually about three ninety-pound bales a day), six apples, six carrots, six loaves of bread, and vitamin and mineral supplements. Every other day they also eat about five pounds of **hydroponic** grass, a special nutritious grass grown at the zoo in water instead of soil.

Rhinos eat about thirty pounds of grain, one to three bales of hay, six potatoes, and six carrots daily. Every third day, they also eat twenty pounds of hydroponic grass, and sometimes they get a special treat of mulberry branches or other **browse** (leaves and twigs).

It's important for elephants and rhinos to be accustomed to eating foods such as apples and potatoes. This is because, should they ever become ill, medication can be hidden inside these types of foods and hand-fed to the animals by their keepers.

Fruits and vegetables are purchased for primates and birds. Throughout the warm months of the year, keepers collect browse from the trees in the zoo. This is frozen and saved for use later in the year. Each zoo building has a spotlessly clean kitchen used for preparing animal meals. The keepers prepare the meals following directions written on a blackboard that detail each animal's diet.

Where do the animals sleep at night when it's cold?

Almost all of the zoo's animals are brought indoors to sleep at night whether it is cold or not. Most often, their indoor quarters are connected to their outdoor exhibit area. Taking the animals in at night protects them from bad weather and gives the keepers a chance to observe them closely and make sure they are feeling well. If they are ill, one of the zoo's veterinarians will be called in.

In the winter, some animals—such as lions, zebras, elephants, and giraffes—are not allowed to go outdoors at all. This is because they come from Africa, Asia, or other warm parts of the world, and cannot withstand the cold temperatures. Other animals, those that are native to cooler northern climates, stay outdoors in the winter. These include bison and bears, which have long, thick coats of fur to keep them warm.

In the summer, when the temperature often rises above 90° Fahrenheit in New York, bears help keep themselves cool by remaining fairly inactive and by swimming in the large pools of cool water in their exhibits. Reptiles, many of which come from very hot climates, live year-round in exhibits where the temperature is kept over 90° F.

Animals often live longer in zoos than they would in the wild. This is because they are fed nutritious meals, receive medical care when needed, and are protected from other animals that might harm them.

Are all the people who work at the Bronx Zoo animal keepers?

There are all kinds of jobs at the zoo. Some involve the care of animals, and others involve the administration and upkeep of the zoo itself. Each department at the zoo is supervised by a curator, and many keepers take care of the animals on a day-to-day basis. But many other kinds of jobs exist at the zoo in such departments as Graphics, Photography, Education, and Publicity, as well as the zoo's Animal Health Center.

Are there any teachers at the zoo?

The zoo employs several full-time teachers in its education department. Among other things, they create teaching materials, offer classes for children and adults, and run a zoo camp and a zookeeping internship program in the summer. For course catalogs, you can write to: New York Zoological Society, Bronx Zoo, Education Department, Bronx, New York 10460.

What does a zookeeper do?

Keepers are responsible for such things as cleaning exhibits, preparing food and feeding animals, and observing animals to make sure they're in good health. If a birth is expected, keepers often take turns keeping watch over the pregnant female so that a veterinarian can be reached in case of an emergency. When babies are born, keepers have to take notes on the behavior of the babies, their parents, and any other animals sharing the exhibit. Whenever new animals are added to an exhibit, it's important to make sure they adjust.

How are the animals and their exhibits cleaned?

Each morning before the zoo opens to the public, zookeepers are hard at work cleaning the exhibits. Most of the time the animals are transferred to a holding area next to their exhibit, so that the keepers can work quickly without disturbing the animals or being in any danger. Cleaning may include hosing down floors and walls,

*At the Animal Health Center, a health technician bottle-feeds
a small African antelope called a duiker.*

scrubbing artificial rocks and plants, and washing glass windows. After the exhibit is thoroughly cleaned, the animals are returned.

Most animals take care of their own hygiene. Birds such as ducks, flamingos, and penguins bathe in the pools and lakes in their exhibit areas. Condors and bluebirds use their beaks to clean their feathers instead of bathing. Large cats, like lions, clean their fur with their rough tongues, just as housecats do. Rhinos take mud baths, digging mud holes to lie in to cool themselves and keep their sensitive skin from drying out.

A few animals, however, need to be cleaned by their keepers. For example, elephants are bathed by hand with soap and water, and then given a hose shower, which they love!

Asian elephants love water and swimming, and also the soap-and-water baths their keepers regularly give them.

Do the keepers brush the animals' teeth?

It isn't necessary for wild animals to have their teeth brushed. The foods they eat usually keep them in good dental health. But if an animal must be anesthetized (put into a deep sleep) for some medical reason, the veterinarian will usually take care of any necessary dental work at that time.

What do you need to study to become a zookeeper?

Most people who work at modern zoos study science, especially biology, in high school and college. Many colleges offer courses in zoology as well. Because the care of zoo animals is very complex, advanced education for keepers and curators is required. For information on jobs available in zoos, you can write to the American Association of Zoological Parks and Aquariums (AAZPA), Oglebay Park, Wheeling, West Virginia 26003. Ask for the brochure called "Careers."

What does a zoo veterinarian do?

A veterinarian is a doctor who treats animals. The zoo veterinarian's job is not just to take care of animals when they are sick; it is also to make sure the animals are kept healthy, and to plan for any special care needed by baby animals born at the zoo. Helping the Bronx Zoo's veterinarians with these tasks is a staff of pathologists, radiologists, and other medical technicians and

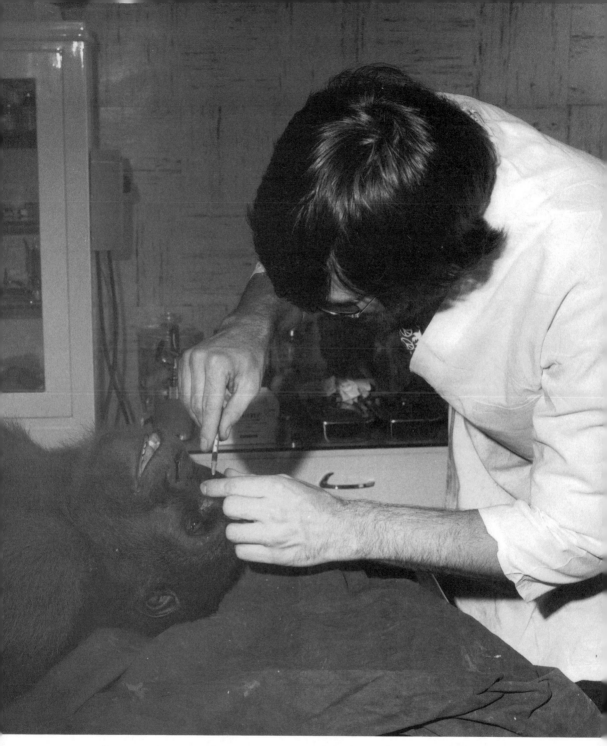

In the zoo's hospital, the late veterinarian Dr. Emil Dolensek performs a delicate operation on a gorilla's eye.

interns, as well as a full-time nutritionist. The zoo opened a large new health center in 1985. It has operating rooms with examination tables small enough for rodents and large enough for elephants. There are also fully equipped laboratories, and quarters for the animals to rest in until they are well enough to return to their exhibits.

How does the veterinarian know when an animal is sick? What happens when a giraffe gets a sore throat?

The keepers are usually the first people to be aware of any health problems among the animals. Large, hoofed animals, like Roosevelt elk, American bison, and Père David deer, are observed in the morning as they are released into their exhibits, and again in the evening when they are taken off-exhibit to be fed. The daily feeding routine is one way in which the staff can control and monitor the health of every animal.

A giraffe can't tell anyone if its throat feels sore, but if an animal isn't feeling well, its keepers will notice and call in one of the veterinarians. Tests will be done to determine what is making the animal ill, and then the proper medicine is prescribed.

What happens when an animal dies?

The bodies of all animals that die at the zoo are studied carefully. The doctors perform an examination on the body called a necropsy, and keep a record of the results. The findings of these examinations may help the veterinarians keep other animals of the same species healthy. Sometimes important organs, like the heart or liver, are preserved so that they can be studied later. The remains of the dead animals are then reduced to ashes. The Animal Health Center also keeps on file records showing the date every animal arrives at the zoo, the animal's date of birth, any illness it may have had in the past, and any special notes on its diet or health.

Does the zoo train any of its animals?

The zoo prefers to keep its wild animals as close to their natural wild state as possible. However, it is sometimes important to train some of the animals so that they can be cared for properly. For that reason, elephants are trained to do "tricks" like lifting a foot or sitting down on command, which is useful if a veterinarian needs to examine them.

What kinds of plants do you have at the zoo? Do they need any special care?

The Bronx Zoo is in a natural forest that has a great many native trees. The kind and location of each tree is kept on file in a computer at the zoo. The landscaping of exhibits is coordinated by curators and exhibit designers. Many exhibits require special plants from various parts of the world. These are often purchased from other states or countries. Sometimes they are grown in greenhouses at the zoo. The Himalayan Highlands has over forty species of special plants, many of them native to Asia. Bamboo is planted around the zoo for some of the animals, and browse is grown in an outdoor nursery and picked straight from trees for leaf-eating animals like the proboscis monkey. In some exhibits, artificial plants and trees are used instead of real ones. This is because either there is not enough natural light or space for the trees, or because the animals in the exhibit might eat the plants if they were within reach. You may have seen wire netting around some of the tree trunks at the zoo. This helps to keep the animals from eating all the bark, which would eventually harm the trees. All of the gardening and plant maintenance at the zoo is the responsibility of the Assistant Director of Exhibition.

Does the Bronx Zoo have a professional designer for the new habitats it builds, or does the staff do the designing?

Exhibits designed at the zoo represent the joint effort of a large team of contractors and the zoo's staff of professional designers. When an existing building is remodeled at the zoo, the remodeling involves updating existing mechanical systems, and creating new display areas for the animals that will be housed there.

In 1986, the zoo opened its Himalayan Highlands exhibit. Before building any part of the display, the zoo staff carefully studied the native environments of the animals they were planning to house. They then set about to duplicate those environments as closely as possible, blending artificial rocks and trees with natural ones, and using barely noticeable glass and wire rather than bars and cages to contain the animals. For JungleWorld, workers built replicas of vast Asian tropical forests, mangrove swamps, and desertlike scrub lands.

Creating a naturalistic exhibit requires planning, creativity, and teamwork, so that the exhibit will be a safe and secure place for the animals, and so that visitors will be able to see what it's like to be part of the animals' world. For some animals, such as giraffes, wolves, elk, and monkeys, large exhibits must be created so that these animals can live with members of their families or groups as they would in nature.

Can people buy animals from the zoo?

No. Zoo animals are not for sale to the public. All of the animals at the zoo are wild, and it is the zoo's policy that wild animals should not be kept as pets. A wild animal requires special care in terms of food, habitat, and veterinary attention, and does not make a good—or safe—pet.

Mammals

What is a mammal?

An animal must have two things to be considered a mammal: fur or hair on its body, and organs called mammary glands with which it feeds milk to its young. Mammals breathe air and have backbones, well-developed brains, and four-chambered hearts. Almost all mammals give birth to live young, and are able to keep their bodies at a constant temperature no matter how hot or cold their surroundings may be. (Animals that can control their own body temperature internally with the heat produced from the food they eat are called **endothermic,** or "warm-blooded.") As with all rules, there are a few exceptions, which we will talk about later.

Are human beings mammals?

Yes, they are. In fact, there are more human beings than any other large mammal.

Human beings are considered one of the "higher" **primates,** along with monkeys and apes. The higher primates have more highly developed vision and bigger brains, and are larger than most other primates. Records of primates on earth go back about 70 million years. Records of human beings go back only about 70,000 to 300,000 years. Considering that there have been animals on earth for several hundred million years, primates are fairly recent arrivals.

How many different kinds of mammals are there?

There are between four thousand and five thousand species of mammals living in the world. Mammal species can be very different from one another. The blue whale, for instance, can weigh up to 143 tons and grow to one hundred feet in length, while the tiny pygmy shrew, only one inch long, weighs just a fraction of an ounce.

Some mammals are **terrestrial,** living mostly on land; some are **aquatic,** living in or around water; and some are **arboreal,** spending most of their time in trees. Each group of animals has a body type that's specially **adapted,** or suited, to the environment it inhabits and the food it eats. Means of **locomotion,** or movement, vary in different species from running to gliding, swimming, leaping, **brachiating** (swinging from branch to branch in a hand-over-hand movement), burrowing, and flying.

Some land animals, called **ungulates,** have hooves or hard coverings on their toes (cattle, deer, horses); others, called **rodents** (such as squirrels, mice, and porcupines), have long, sharp incisor teeth with which they gnaw food and other substances.

There are even toothless mammals, like the anteater. And some mammals, such as the Australian kangaroo and the American opossum, are **marsupials,** and raise their tiny newborns in pouches.

Aquatic mammals have bodies that are streamlined, and often flippered, to give them mobility in the water. These mammals live in rivers and oceans but must come to the surface of the water to breathe air. They include whales, dolphins, seals, sea lions, otters, and beavers.

Only one type of mammal flies, and that is the bat. Of the 4,000-plus mammal species in the world, about 1,700 are rodent species and 900 are bat species.

Is there a difference between human hair and animal hair?

No, not really. Fur and hair are made of the same substances. Even whiskers and porcupine quills are forms of hair or fur.

All mammals—even such animals as whales and elephants—have at least some hair or fur. Hair covers the body, keeps it warm, and protects the skin. This covering can **camouflage** an animal by helping the animal to blend in with its surroundings, or help animals of the same species find and attract each other.

Where do mammals live? How do they protect their territories?

Mammals make their homes all over the world—in deserts, mountains, forests, plains, and seas. They can live in warm *and* cold regions of the world because their hair, fur, or fatty blubber helps protect them from the elements.

Some animals mark off a certain amount of **territory,** or land, within which they hunt, mate, or raise their young. To keep other animals out of their territory, they may use scent marks or make certain sounds. For example, tigers spray trees with strong-smelling urine and make deep scratch marks with their claws, while small apes, called gibbons, make very loud hooting noises.

What kinds of foods do mammals eat?

The feeding habits of mammal species vary widely. **Carnivorous** mammals, such as polar bears, lions, wolves, and anteaters, eat the flesh of other mammals, or eat other animals like fish, insects, or **invertebrates** (animals without backbones). An animal that preys on other animals is called a **predator.** Carnivores are predators; many have enlarged canine teeth that they use for tearing flesh.

Prey animals (those that are hunted by predators) are often **herbivorous.** Herbivores, like cows, deer, and rabbits, eat only plant matter, such as grass, seeds, nuts, fruits, berries, and bark. Almost all of the large herbivorous mammals are ungulates. Ungulates have large molar teeth for grinding; their food must be well chewed before it reaches their stomachs for digesting. Rodents (mice, rats, squirrels) eat plant matter, but they don't chew their food, they gnaw it. The word *rodent* actually means "gnawing animal." Rodents must gnaw or else their long front incisor teeth will overgrow to the point that they cannot properly open their mouths to eat, and they will starve to death.

A third type of mammal is **omnivorous.** The omnivore's diet consists of both plants and animals. Human beings, raccoons, and many types of bears are omnivores.

Some animals are specialized eaters. Koalas, for instance, eat only eucalyptus leaves, and giant pandas eat bamboo almost exclusively. Black-footed ferrets, which once roamed America's prairies in large numbers, eat prairie dogs and just about nothing else. A limited diet of mainly one kind of food can become a serious problem for many animals—especially when that one food is in short supply.

How do mammals find and catch their food?

Think of a cheetah, which is a carnivorous African mammal. It has a streamlined, sleek body, sharp claws which help it to catch its prey, strong teeth for tearing flesh, and the ability to run faster for short distances than any other land animal. Most carnivores have keen eyesight and a good sense of smell to help them track down prey. They have what's called **binocular vision,** which means their two eyes face forward. Binocular vision helps an animal hunt by giving it a sense of **depth perception,** enabling it to see three dimensionally and allowing it to focus both eyes on the same object. Herbivorous prey animals, on the other hand, generally have **monocular vision:** Their eyes are set far apart on either side of their head so that they can see in two directions at once. This broader range of vision helps them spot predators more easily, but does not enable them to hunt.

Some animals, like the lion, the killer whale, and the wolf, hunt in packs and share their catches. Some, like the tiger, hunt

Wolves are highly social animals that live in family groups or packs, often hunting together to capture prey.

alone. The advantage to hunting in packs is that teamwork can make the hunt easier, and larger prey can be brought down. Solitary hunting requires more individual energy, and often results in smaller catches, but the food does not have to be divided up among many mouths, as in pack hunting.

Now think about which animals the lion hunts. Prey animals, such as antelopes or zebras, are well adapted for fleeing quickly to escape from predators. This means that they have fast reflexes and can run swiftly. They usually have a good sense of smell so that they can detect predators nearby, and will often make warning sounds or signals of some kind to give others of their own species the chance to escape the danger, too. Other prey animals, like rabbits, may defend themselves by freezing when they realize a predator is nearby: Their fur color is often similar to their surroundings (a brown rabbit on the forest floor), and this helps camouflage them so well that they often cannot be detected by the predators.

Prey animals must eat, too. Most of them do not have to catch their food, though, since, as we mentioned before, many prey animals eat plants.

All of an animal's special qualities, or adaptations, help it to survive in its environment. Carnivorous marine mammals, like seals and sea lions, feed on fish. They have flippers, which are like legs adapted for efficient swimming. They have whiskers, which they use to detect fish swimming nearby in the darkness of their underwater habitat. Many species of monkeys live in trees, and use their strong arms to propel themselves from branch to branch and tree to tree, where they find food, shelter, and places to breed and raise young. Some herbivorous animals are extremely large and strong. Elephants are one such animal. They are so immense that they have no natural enemies—except people.

How many different types of elephants are there? Where do they live, and how old do they live to be?

There are two species of elephant—the Asian or Indian, and the African. The Asian is smaller than the African, has smaller ears and tusks, and has lighter-colored and softer skin.

Elephants use their ears like giant fans to keep their bodies free of flies and cool, since they have no sweat glands to help them release body heat. Elephants travel in single file, have small but alert eyes and a good sense of smell and hearing, and feel at home both in the water and on land. A mature African elephant can grow as large as eleven feet tall at the shoulder and weigh up to 12,000 pounds, while an Asian male can grow to nine or ten feet (seven feet for a female).

The Asian elephant has a small projection or "lip" at the end of its trunk to help it feel and grasp things; the African has two of these lips. The elephant uses its trunk to pick up anything—from an enormous log to a tiny piece of food. The trunk is actually a long nose that is **prehensile,** which means that, like a finger, it can encircle and grasp things. The trunk is used for many things: touching and smelling, carrying food and water to the mouth, lifting another elephant out of the mud, greeting friends, and for sand and dust bathing. Elephants have very sensitive skin (despite its thickness), and must give themselves dust, sand, or mud baths to protect themselves from sunburn and insect bites. Except for the long tuft at the end of their tails, elephants have little hair. This is an adaptation for losing heat, which is important to large mammals living in hot, tropical areas.

An elephant's tusks are actually elongated upper incisor teeth that continue to grow all through life. In the African species, both males and females have tusks; in the Asian, only the males have tusks. Many elephants have been killed by hunters for their ivory tusks, reducing their populations severely. Though steps have been taken to outlaw this, in many places illegal hunting still goes on. The only other teeth elephants have are enormous molars. They have six sets of molars in their jaws, and when one set wears away, another moves down to take its place. When the last set of molars is gone, the elephant can no longer eat, and eventually dies.

In the wild, Asian elephants live in India, Sri Lanka, and Southeast Asia. The African elephant lives in both forested areas and

A highly intelligent animal, the Asian elephant uses its long trunk for eating, bathing, touching, smelling, and greeting other elephants.

open grasslands called **savannahs.** Though they once ranged all through Africa, their numbers have been greatly reduced, and they now are confined to the tropics. Efforts are being made to reserve land for them in national parks, so the species will not become extinct.

Elephants are very social animals and live in herds, or family groups, that contain about ten or so related females (cows) and their young. When a female gives birth, she is aided by other females (her sisters or other close relatives), who act as **midwives.** The female's **gestation** period, or the amount of time a mother elephant is pregnant with her young, is from twenty to twenty-six months. Elephants usually give birth to one calf. The newborn is about three feet tall and weighs about two hundred pounds. The midwives stay close by until the newborn is on its feet and nursing, and able to follow its mother. A baby elephant drinks about ten quarts of milk a day.

Elephants can live to sixty-five or seventy years of age. Herds are led by the oldest and most experienced females, called the matriarchs. Elephants spend most of their day feeding. They eat up to three hundred pounds of food daily—grass, leaves, plants, and bark—and shade themselves in the forest during the hottest part of the day. Elephants drink over forty gallons of water a day, and they love to swim. In times of drought, the matriarch's guidance is very important, for she, being the oldest, will know best where to lead her family to find water and food.

Male elephants (bulls) live either in their own herds or by themselves. They leave their mothers when they are ten to fifteen years old and are fully able to fend for themselves.

Elephants have good memories and are highly intelligent. They communicate by touch (using their trunks to stay in contact with one another, especially mothers and baby elephants) and by sound (long-distance trumpeting helps members of a family find one another). They are capable of many emotions, and are said to mourn the loss of their relatives. At the Bronx Zoo, we have Asian elephants.

Why do giraffes have such long necks?

The giraffe's body is perfectly adapted to reach high foliage, such as the leaves that are found high up on acacia trees in the African savannah. Giraffes also have long, black, prehensile tongues, which can be extended up to one and a half feet and wrapped around the thorny acacia leaves to gather them to eat.

Do giraffes have any natural enemies?

Their main predators are lions. Baby giraffes, and adult giraffes that are lowering their bodies for a drink of water, are most at risk from lion attacks. But giraffes can defend themselves with swift kicks from their powerful legs and hooved feet. Also, giraffes have excellent hearing and a good sense of sight and smell, to alert them to possible dangers. Babies are born about six feet tall and fall that far to the ground during birth, since their mothers give birth standing up. Babies are able to run with the herd soon after birth.

There is only one species of giraffe, made up of eight different races, each with its own distinctive pattern of spots. The eight

races are: Nigerian, reticulated, Baringo, Masai, Kordofan, Nubian, Thornicrofts, Angolan, and Cape giraffes. At the Bronx Zoo, we have a herd of Baringo giraffes which originate from East Africa.

What do koalas look like? How big do they get? Who are their relatives?

Koalas are marsupials—pouched animals—with gray to tawny coats and white patches on their chins, chests, front limbs, and ears. They are usually twenty-eight to thirty inches long, and weigh twelve to twenty-six pounds. Koalas inhabit the eucalypt forest in east Australia, and are highly specialized eaters, feeding on only a few different types of eucalyptus leaves as their complete diet.

In the early 1900s, koalas almost became extinct, mainly because early settlers hunted them so heavily for their fur. By the early part of the twentieth century, though, hunting was banned and the species was saved.

Koalas are **nocturnal,** live in trees, and have thick fur, large paws, strong claws for climbing, and **opposable** first and second **digits.** Digits are similar to fingers. Opposable digits are ones that can be placed against one or more of the other digits. (On a human, the opposable thumb can be moved against all of the other fingers.) Opposable digits help koalas climb easily.

The female's pouch opens to the back. One young weighing less than one-fiftieth of an ounce is born and attaches itself to one of the female's nipples in the pouch. The mother **weans** the baby

With their exceptionally long legs and necks, giraffes are the tallest land mammals in the world and can grow up to nineteen feet high.

off milk after five months, at first feeding it partially digested leaves. The young become fully independent at eleven months. Koalas do little socializing, except the young, which are quite playful with each other.

Koalas, which are related to opossums, kangaroos, and wombats, are slow moving, sleep eighteen hours a day, and begin feeding at dusk. Adults eat over a pound of food daily, getting most of the water they need from the leaves they eat. Their teeth consist of molars and premolars only, since koalas only need to grind up leaves. The life expectancy of a koala is thirteen years.

What kind of bears do you have at the Bronx Zoo? Do bears hibernate in winter? How big do they grow, and what do they eat?

At the Bronx Zoo, we have polar and Kodiak bears. Kodiaks are related to grizzly or brown bears, but live only on Kodiak Island and other Alaskan islands. In addition to these two species of large bears, there are also the American black bear and four smaller species: the Asian black, the sloth, the sun, and the spectacled bears.

Polar bears are the largest land-dwelling carnivores in the world, but even a polar bear may rely on vegetation if animal prey is scarce. Polar bears are well adapted for life in the frigid cold, and spend a great deal of time in and around arctic waters. Their white coats help to camouflage them as they hunt for prey (mainly seals, fish, and walruses) in the snow and ice, and the fur on the soles of their feet and on their toes helps keep them warm and surefooted on the ice. They have three or four inches of blubber

Polar bears give birth to one or two cubs, who need parental care for several years until they are able to fend for themselves.

under their skin for insulation, hollow fur that allows the sun's rays to penetrate, and black skin under their fur to absorb heat. A male polar bear can grow as large as sixteen to seventeen hundred pounds, and a female to a thousand pounds. Polar bears live up to twenty-five years in the wild, thirty-five in captivity.

All other species of bears are either omnivores or herbivores. The grizzly bear (males can grow as large as 1,000 pounds, and females 450 pounds) will eat anything from rodents, fish, and deer, to tubers, berries, and succulent plants. The sun, or Malayan, bear is a good climber and spends much of its time feeding and resting in trees. The Asian black bear also **forages** in trees. The sloth bear is nocturnal, hangs upside down like a sloth, and uses its flexible lips to suck up insects. The spectacled bear gets its name from the round white markings around each of its eyes, which look like spectacles or eyeglasses.

Most bears give birth to one or two young weighing less than a pound or two each. The cubs remain with the mother for several years while they grow and learn to fend for themselves. All of the bear species **den** in the winter except the sun and spectacled bears, and male polar bears. Of those that do rest in lairs, only the brown and American black actually **hibernate.** Pregnant female polar bears become **dormant** but do not hibernate, and the sloth bear dens for privacy but does not become dormant.

Scientists have recently determined that the giant panda of China is actually in the bear family, not in the raccoon family as had formerly been believed. (See "Endangered Species" for more on the panda.)

What kind of dog is a prairie dog?

Though it may yelp like a dog, a prairie dog is a rodent and not a dog at all. Prairie dogs are small, buff-colored animals that live in the western part of the United States. They build large communal burrows (called "towns") shared by up to fifteen animals, each having its own private den. When there is danger, one prairie dog will sound a two-syllable alarm call or bark to warn all nearby to take cover. Prairie dogs may become dormant— going into almost complete hibernation—during extreme cold. They feed on grass and insects.

The Children's Zoo in the Bronx Zoo has a colony of prairie dogs, and visitors can go underground and imagine what it would be like to live in a prairie dog burrow.

Are hippopotamuses related to rhinoceroses?

No, they are not. The African hippopotamus lives in herds, browsing on water plants or swimming during the day in large rivers and lakes. At night, it comes up on land to eat grass. Females live together, surrounded by males which have individual territories that they protect fiercely.

Despite their thick skin and bulky size (they can weigh up to four tons), hippos are good swimmers. Their nostrils and mouths seal closed when underwater, and they can stay submerged for long periods of time simply by keeping the tops of their heads out of the water to breathe. They sometimes walk or swim along the river bottom, and can stay completely underwater for several minutes at a time. Because they have been hunted heavily, hippos have learned to rest in places where they can stay hidden and protected. In addition to the African, there is also a pygmy hippopotamus, one-tenth its size.

The five rhino species—the black rhino and white rhino of Africa, and the Indian, Sumatran, and Javan found in Asia—all have big horns on the centers of their heads. These horns easily distinguish them from hippos.

The African black rhino, whose habitat is now limited to East African preserves, has two horns. The Indian has only one. Rhinos can weigh up to two tons. Like hippos, they have thick skin and hooved feet. They are solitary animals, mostly nocturnal, and their diet consists of leaves, twigs, and plants. Rhinos enjoy bathing in mud because it helps protect their skin. Rhinos can be very aggressive animals, and are not believed to be very intelligent.

The other species of two-horned rhinos are the white, or square-lipped, and the smaller Sumatran. The white is **diurnal** (active in the daytime), and though quite large—up to four tons—it is much more peaceful than the black. There is also a one-horned, extremely rare Javan rhinoceros.

Rhinos have been hunted for hundreds of years because some people believe that rhino horns have value as medicine. There is no scientific proof that this is so. At the Bronx Zoo, we have Indian rhinos and pygmy hippos.

Why do tigers and zebras have stripes?

Tigers hunt in tall grasses, crouching low and then springing forward as far as fifteen feet to capture their prey. Their vertical stripes camouflage them perfectly—the light and dark markings blending with the grass around them. Tigers rest in the forest during the day seeking shade from the heat, and in the evening stalk their prey (ox, deer, boar). The Siberian tiger is the variety we have at the Bronx Zoo.

Zebras are native to Africa, and were once called "horse-tigers" because of their stripes. Zebras are not hunters (on the contrary, they are herbivorous grazing animals, often preyed on by lions), so their stripes must serve some other purpose. It is believed that the stripes help the individuals in a herd to find one another. Another theory is that the stripes act as a kind of disruptive coloration, helping to camouflage the animals. You can imagine that it might be difficult for a predator to single out one individual to attack from a fast-moving pack of zebra stripes. Just as no two humans have the same fingerprints, no two zebras have the exact same set of stripes.

There are three species of zebra—common, or Burchell's;

mountain (existing only in small numbers in reserves); and Grévy's. The Grévy's are the largest species, and are the type we have on exhibit at the Bronx Zoo.

Which members of the cat family are the "big cats"?

All members of the cat family are carnivores, or flesh eaters, and are skilled hunters. But the "great" or "big" cats—lions, tigers, leopards, and jaguars—are the best hunters of them all. They use their sharp claws and teeth, keen eyesight and sense of smell, padded toes (for quiet approaches), sensitive whiskers (for feeling their way at night), and tremendous strength to capture their prey. What distinguishes the big cats from the other members of the cat family is not just their size and strength, but also their vocalizations, or the sounds they make. Big cats all roar, but cannot purr. All of the other cats purr, growl, snarl, and spit, but are unable to roar. The other cats include mountain lions, clouded leopards, and cheetahs.

How many different types of tigers are there? Do they attack people?

There are believed to be seven types of tiger in Asia—all variations of the same species. Since tigers are very endangered and their numbers are small, it is not known if all of the seven varieties still exist. They are: Siberian, Bengal, Caspian, Sumatran, Corbett's, Javan, and Chinese tiger. Fifty years ago there were over one hundred thousand tigers; today there are less than six thousand. They have been heavily hunted for their fur, and have also died out from loss of forest habitat and food source.

Tigers hunt by themselves, preying on ox, boar, peacock, cattle, deer, and even fish. They often travel fifteen miles in search of prey. Tigers fear humans, and knowing they are no match for our weapons, will rarely attack unless threatened or provoked. In those rare instances where tigers have become man-eaters, it is usually a situation where natural prey is scarce or the tiger has become old and lost much of its strength and hunting ability.

Why do lions live in prides?

Of all the big cats, lions are the only ones that are social. They live together in family groups, called prides, of up to thirty-five individuals. All other cats are solitary, meaning that they live

You can tell a male African lion (top) from a female by the ruff of fur around its head, called a mane, and by its larger body size.

alone except during mating, and when a mother is raising her cubs. Tigers, leopards, and jaguars are nocturnal and live in swamps and forests, while lions are active during the daytime and live in open grasslands.

The males in a lion pride work together to protect their territory and to keep outside males from taking over their pride. Hunting is done by several lions together, and catches are usually shared by all pride members. Adult males generally do not participate in the hunt. Almost all of the lions in existence today live in Africa. There is a small population of Asian lions which live in a reserve in India.

Are duck-billed platypuses ducks or mammals?
What do they eat, and where do they live?
Are any other animals related to the platypus?

The duck-billed platypus is a semi-aquatic, **oviparous** (or egg-laying) mammal. Because most mammals give birth to live young rather than lay eggs, the platypus is quite unusual. Pregnant females build dry, grass-lined burrows in the riverbank, and lay two eggs in them. Platypuses have bills like ducks, which they use to sift through mud or sand on the river bottoms to find the shrimp, **larvae,** earthworms, and tadpoles they feed on. The platypus weighs two to five pounds. It has short, dense, reddish fur, webbed paws with claws, and a flat tail which it uses like a boat rudder to guide itself through the water. Platypuses spend most of their day in their burrows, and only a few hours in the water.

In addition to the platypus, the other type of egg-laying mammal is the echidna, or spiny anteater. There are long- and short-

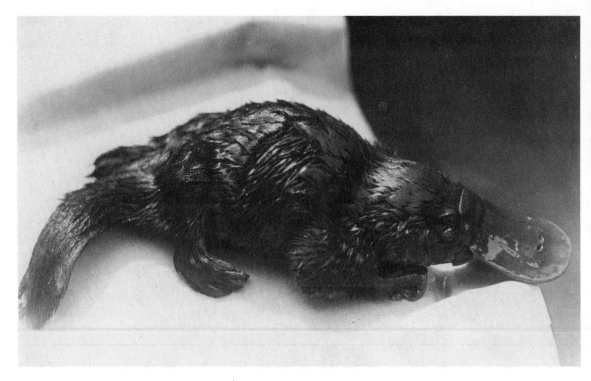

The duck-billed platypus is a small oviparous mammal that has some characteristics in common with both reptiles and birds.

beaked echidnas, both of which are terrestrial and have long spines on their bodies. The long-beaked echidnas feed mainly on earthworms; the short-beaked ones on insects, which they catch with their long, sticky tongues. Just before the breeding season, the female echidna develops a marsupial-type pouch on her stomach. She lays one or two eggs, and bends her body so that the eggs move into the pouch, where they are hatched. To defend itself, the echidna will burrow into the ground, leaving its sharp spines sticking up. Echidnas live in Australia, Tasmania, and New Guinea. Platypuses live in eastern and southern Australia and Tasmania— at home in both freezing and tropical waters.

The platypus and the echidna are both monotremes. *Mono-*

treme literally means "one hole." Like reptiles, all monotremes have only one hole—the cloaca—through which wastes are passed. Platypuses are similar to reptiles in that they have a cloaca, and they are similar to birds in that they lay eggs and have beaks. But they have fur and mammary glands—feeding their young milk once they are hatched—and this decidedly makes them mammals.

Monotremes and certain members of the shrew family are the only venomous (poisonous) mammals. Among the mono-tremes, only the male platypus has a functioning **venom** gland. It is located behind the knee and connected to the back of the ankle. Monotremes are ancient-type animals that have survived from long ago. The exact origin of these animals is not known, because scientists have found no fossil remains to study.

Comparing monotremes to the two other groups of mammals, we find that marsupials (kangaroos, wombats, opossums) give birth to very immature young and then nurse them in a pouch, and **placentals** give birth to live young that are connected to their mothers before they are born by a placenta and umbilical cord, which provides the growing **embryo** with food and oxygen. Pla-cental animals compose a broad spectrum of the mammal world, from mice to hedgehogs, horses, lions, monkeys, apes, and humans.

Birds

What makes a bird a bird?

A bird is any animal with feathers. Birds have many qualities in common with mammals and reptiles, but it is their feathers that set them apart in the animal world.

How do birds fly?

Birds vary in size from those weighing several ounces (hummingbirds), to twenty-five pounds (condors), to over three hundred pounds (ostriches). The weight of a bird determines the kind of flying it does—flapping, gliding, soaring—or if it can fly at all.

Some of the features that enable birds to fly include: a compact body of rigid, hollow bones; an inflexible, shock-resistant spine; a flexible neck with from eleven to twenty-five **vertebrae;** a large breastbone, or **keel;** very strong muscles attached to the keel called **pectoral** muscles; and feathers. Every part of a bird's body is designed for strength and lightness.

Birds have many kinds of feathers, each for a different purpose. There are primary and secondary flight feathers on the wings; covert feathers to shape, insulate, and protect the wings; tail flight feathers; contour feathers, which provide the outer shape; and down feathers for warmth. The shaft (central spine) of all feathers is made of **keratin,** the same horny substance that makes up our fingernails and hair. Just as hair does, feathers fall out and are replaced. Feathers are usually **molted,** or shed, once a year and regrow in about three to seven weeks. Flying birds usually do not molt all at once, for then they wouldn't be able to fly. Birds with other means of movement, like penguins, which swim, do molt all their flight feathers at one time. A small songbird, like a robin or a warbler, has over one thousand feathers; a duck has about twelve thousand; and a swan has twenty-five thousand.

A bird continuously cleans, or preens, its feathers with its bill, so that it will be warm, protected, and ready to fly.

The upper surface of any bird's wing forms an arch, the shape necessary for flying. Skin connects all the parts of the wing, and feathers grow out of the skin. Each feather has tiny barbs which interlock so that no air can pass through or around an individual feather. A bird must continually care for its feathers by **preening** (using its beak to arrange and clean the feathers), so it will always be ready and able to fly. The force of the air, both below and especially above the wing, combined with the angle of the wing and the energy with which it is flapped, produce flight.

Do birds have teeth? What do they eat?

Birds do not have any teeth, an adaptation that helps keep them light for flight, so it is necessary for a bird's bill or beak to be an efficient eating tool. The size and shape of a particular bill "fits" the food that that bird eats. Here are some examples:

A short, thick beak, found on birds like nuthatches and cardinals, is used for cracking seeds. A short but thinner beak, such as the robin's, is designed to catch insects.

Strong, hooked beaks, like those of owls, hawks, and eagles, are used for tearing up prey such as rodents and small birds. Vultures and condors use their sharp, hooked beaks to rip up **carrion,** the flesh of dead animals.

Long, narrow beaks can be used for probing in flowers for nectar or insects. Hummingbirds and sunbirds have these kinds of beaks. The longer and pointier bills of herons and egrets are used for searching in the mud for small crabs, fish, and frogs. A long, pointy, and slightly thicker bill is used by the oystercatcher as a chisel to pry open oysters.

*A tall, long-necked American egret uses its
sharp bill to hunt for food in shallow waters.*

A flat, rounded bill with strainerlike edges is used by ducks to remove plants from the water. A similar beak, with saw-toothed edges, is utilized by diving ducks such as mergansers to grab hold of fish.

Birds have other adaptations for food gathering and digestion as well. The **crop,** a storage area about halfway down the **esophagus,** or food pipe, allows birds to eat more than they can digest immediately and carry the extra food away with them. The stomach of a bird has a special part called the **gizzard,** where hard materials like pebbles or sand help to crush the food. A sandpiper or other beach dweller may have almost half of its stomach filled with sand.

A bird's tongue is specially adapted to help with feeding, too. Macaws have hard tongues that help push meaty nuts out of their shells. A hummingbird has a tubelike tongue for sipping nectar out of flowers. And woodpeckers have barbed tongues that help them remove insects from hiding places in trees.

What makes birds able to live in different kinds of places around the world?

If we examine some of the different habitats in which birds are found, we can discover which adaptations help them to survive. Since most of the earth is covered by water, it is natural that many species of birds live on, in, or near bodies of water. Wading birds have very long legs so that their feathers do not get wet while they are hunting along the water's edge. Herons have long toes so they don't sink into the mud. The jacanas' long toes allow them to walk on top of lily pads and other vegetation.

Birds that swim, such as ducks and gulls, have specialized

feet that are webbed to help push the water. Most birds have oil **glands,** but these are most important to water birds since a coating of oil will help keep their feathers dry. This oil is spread over the feathers during preening. Water birds also have a lot of air-trapping down feathers for warmth. Penguins are an extreme case, since almost all of their thousands of feathers are small down feathers. Antarctic penguins also have a thick layer of fat, or blubber, for extra warmth. Seabirds, which drink a lot of salty water, have developed salt glands near their eyes which remove the harmful salt that builds up in their bodies.

Rain forests and forests of **deciduous** trees (those that lose their leaves every fall) are homes for numerous species of birds. Birds that live in forests often have feathers of various shades of green, which blend in with the trees. Birds have excellent vision, and they see colors. They can easily find not only food but one another. For some, color plays special roles: Ruby-throated hummingbirds prefer nectar from red flowers, and bowerbirds of Australia decorate their **bowers** with colorful items, often blue, to attract females.

Birds that live in the trees also have perching toes, usually two facing front and one or two facing backward. The toes lock into position because the longer tendons in the muscles that curl the toes are stretched when the bird bends its legs. The more it bends the legs, the stronger its grip. This allows the bird to sleep while perching without losing its balance or falling off the branch.

Depending upon the position of the eyes on the head, birds can have a field of vision of almost 360 degrees (a complete circle). Birds that spend most of their time on the ground have to be alert for predators; these birds have more monocular vision, which means they see sideways, with each eye focusing separately. Tree-dwelling birds have better binocular vision, for judging distances as they fly and hunt. Owls, for example, have eyes set forward on their heads, which gives them keen eyesight and good binocular vision so they can accurately spot their prey from a long distance. Owls also locate prey through their good sense of hearing, another important adaptation of forest birds.

In open grasslands and meadows, birds such as partridges, pheasants, and quail use their coloration for camouflage. For further protection, some of these birds can stand quite still when threatened. Others may be well adapted for running, like the flightless ostriches and rheas with their strong legs, hooflike feet, and front-facing toes.

Deserts present many problems for birds, including extreme temperature changes and lack of drinking water. The elf owl hunts during the cooler hours, and in the hottest part of the day sleeps in holes in the cool, damp saguaro cactus. The greater roadrunner is able to get its water from the small reptiles and insects it eats.

Every bird seems to have its own song or call. Why do birds sing?

Songs are one of the most important ways birds communicate with each other. They sing flock-formation songs, calls to get the young to feed, territorial flight songs of male birds, and courtship songs. It is usually the male bird that sings, hoping to attract a female. In forests and jungles, though, where it is harder for birds to find each other, the female sings answering songs to the males. Besides singing, birds also communicate with body language. They use elaborate wing and feather displays for defending territories and attracting mates.

Why do birds build nests? What are nests made of?

The only true purpose of a nest is to protect the eggs that will be laid in it. The size, shape, materials, and location of each nest are as unique as the birds building them.

Some species, like woodpeckers, wrens, kingfishers, and petrels, nest in holes and burrows. The burrowing owl uses a prairie dog burrow for its nest.

Nests are often made of grass and sticks. Gulls, terns, doves, catbirds, and cardinals build such nests. Herons, egrets, ospreys, and eagles make nests of large sticks. An eagle's nest can be as large as nine feet in diameter!

Coots, rails, and gallinules make large platforms out of vegetation for their nests, which are built near lakes, rivers, and streams. The red-winged blackbird actually constructs its nest on tall reeds near the water.

Robins use mud and grass in their nests. Swallows build small mud nests and attach these to the undersides of roofs, bridges, and caves. Ducks and geese use feathers in their nests, and some birds pluck hairs from live mammals and feathers from other birds to line their nests. Birds that live in cities may add refuse, like paper, string, and gum wrappers, to the natural materials in their nests.

All nests are remarkable when you consider that birds make them using only their beaks and feet, but some nests are truly spectacular creations. The drooping and hanging nests of the vireos, orioles, and weavers are woven out of twisted fibers. In the case of the social weaverbirds of Africa, a nest lined with feathers may be one huge construction used by many birds.

Building a nest is a time-consuming, but not necessarily continuous, job. Some birds only work a few hours a day; some don't even work on the nest every day. And the time it takes to finish the job is different for every species. Generally, though, a sparrow takes less than one week to complete a nest, whereas an African hammerhead can take three or four months to finish one. The hammerheads in the World of Birds' African Jungle exhibit at the zoo once took a nest apart to use its sticks and twigs in the construction of another one, which measured about four feet across. You can see that nest building is a serious job for many birds, since a well-constructed nest is the first step in successfully producing young.

Some birds, however, like the turkey vulture, do not construct a nest at all. The female lays her eggs in a hollow tree log. The male emperor penguin **incubates** one egg for two months on top of his webbed foot and underneath a fold of skin on his abdomen. The African jacana lays her eggs on a lily pad.

How many eggs do birds lay? How large are they?

All birds lay eggs, which are incubated, or kept warm, until they hatch. Just as nests are unique, so, too, the size, shape, color, and number of each species' eggs are different. The size of the egg often indicates if a chick will be **precocial,** able to take care of itself right away after birth, or **altricial,** completely dependent on its parents. A large egg often means a more independent chick because there is more yolk to provide nutrition for the growing baby bird. Of course, larger eggs are usually laid by larger species of birds: Hummingbirds lay tiny eggs the size of jellybeans, while ostriches lay large, seven-inch eggs. While most eggs are round or oval, some, like the murre's, are pointed at one end, since they're laid on rocky cliffs and would fall off the edge were they round or oval.

Egg coloration helps provide protection from predators. The egg of an owl can be white because it is hidden in a tree hole, but a tern's egg is laid out in the open on the pebbly ground near the ocean so it is speckled for camouflage. Spots and splotches of color on eggs usually keep them hidden in the shadows up in the

Some birds, like quails, build nests that are just hollows on the ground surrounded by tall grasses.

trees, or help them to blend in with grasses, rocks, or sand on the ground.

The number of eggs a bird lays, called a **clutch,** varies from one egg, laid by flamingos and California condors, to about twenty for ostriches and Mallee fowl. Eagles and loons usually lay two eggs, ducks may lay fifteen, but the average clutch size for an "average" bird is four. The size of the clutch is an indication of how much care the chick will require from incubation until it is ready to leave the nest. Also, the smaller the clutch size, the longer the lifespan of that species.

Some birds sit on their eggs to keep them warm (90° F or more), with males and females taking turns on the nest. In some species, like the chickadees and jays, the female is the only sitter, and the male feeds her. One extreme example is the hornbill: The female is sealed with mud into a nesting cavity in a tree, and the male brings fruit to the tiny opening in the mud for several months during incubation, hatching, and early growth. Later, the female "breaks out" of the nest and rebuilds the covering so she can help the male to feed the rapidly growing chicks.

Some female penguins lay one egg, which is incubated by the male alone while the female returns to the sea to feed. For rheas, it is usually the male bird that covers the eggs and cares for them after hatching.

Mallee fowl of Australia do not sit on their nest mounds at all. The female lays the eggs on the ground, and covers them up with vegetation and soil. During an incubation period of about two months, the male opens and closes the nest to regulate the temperature in it. When the twenty or so eggs hatch, the adults are gone and the chicks must be able to take care of themselves.

In all species, hatching from the egg is the job of the chick alone. It uses its "egg tooth" (just as alligators and turtles do) to break through the shell. After several hours the chick will be separated from the yolk sac, and the adult bird removes the shell from the nest. The pieces of shell must be taken away from the nest area so that they won't attract predators.

Do baby birds need a lot of care?

Some chicks can take care of themselves right after hatching, like the Mallee fowl. Ducks, plovers, and chickens are precocial, but the female birds still **brood** them, keeping them warm and protected for periods of time each day. Others, like hummingbirds, sparrows, and woodpeckers, are altricial and must be cared for by the adults for some time. An extreme example is the condor, which cares for its young for so long that breeding only takes place every other year. Penguins leave their young in the care of other adult birds while they go out to sea to feed and bring back food for their chicks. They find their own young among numerous babies when they return by noticing where the chick was left and recognizing its call.

Where do robins go after the summer?

Robins, like many birds, migrate. When an animal moves from one place to another and then returns, usually because of a change in seasons or weather, it is called **migration.** Birds usually spend the winter in a specific region, and have a different location in which they breed. Neither place can really be called the bird's home, since it spends a great deal of time in both. A robin may breed in New York and spend the colder months in Florida. Some birds, like redhead ducks, migrate from east to west, wintering on the Atlantic coast and nesting in Utah. Others, like jays and chickadees in the western United States, migrate from higher elevations to lower ones, and then back again. Some of the reasons for migration are changes in weather, temperature, food supply, or length of daylight in an area. Many birds seem to migrate, mate, and nest so that they can time the hatching of the chicks with the hatching of a favorite insect they like to eat.

The migration itself is a great accomplishment. The birds must be able to find their way from one fairly exact location to another and back again. Many experiments have been done with different species to try to find out how birds navigate. Some of the things that seem to help are: a bird's ability to see and recognize landmarks along a specific route; use of the sun's position, or the stars in constellations for night migrators; recognition of wind directions for traveling on cloudy days or nights; and "wandering flight," a method used by birds when they are lost and need to get back to the best route. Birds use flight calls to keep in proper position when they migrate in flocks.

Does an ostrich really stick its head in the sand?

Although an ostrich may sometimes appear to be headless, it cannot really put its head under the ground. Ostriches like to eat vegetation and small bugs, so it may look as though there is no head at the end of the bird's long neck as it forages along the ground.

Humboldt penguins from the coast of Peru and Chile are about two feet tall and look a lot like the Magellanic species at the zoo.

Do all penguins come from cold places?
How can they live at the Bronx Zoo
when it gets hot in the summertime?

There are many species of penguins, but only four of them come from the very cold Antarctic. The emperor, chinstrap, Adélie, and gentoo penguins are well adapted for life on the ice and in freezing waters, with their layers of blubber and thousands of downy feathers. In a zoo they require a special exhibit that is temperature controlled to keep them cool. In the Bronx Zoo, a smaller, South American species is exhibited, called the Magellanic penguin. The climate along the coasts of Argentina and Chile where Magellanics live is much less cold, and these penguins have shorter feathers and far less fat. They still need some insulation in the water, but they can certainly adapt to New York summers.

Are all owls nocturnal?

Most owls are nocturnal and do hunt for food at night. They eat small rodents that are active during the night. One exception is the burrowing owl, which lives in the prairies and deserts of North and South America, and hunts in the daytime. Burrowing owls make their homes underground in holes used by prairie dogs and other tunneling animals. These owls eat insects as well as small mammals, including prairie dogs whose homes they share.

Why do flamingos have such a beautiful pink color?

In their natural habitat, flamingos and other pink or orange wading birds get their bright feathers from crystalline substances called **carotenoids,** found in the small, water-dwelling animals they eat, called **crustaceans.** In the zoo, a substance made from carrots is substituted for carotenoids. In addition to crustaceans, flamingos also eat algae, which are aquatic plants.

A flamingo mother feeds her chick in its large cone-shaped nest made from mud and sand.

Why do birds stand on one leg so much?

People shift their weight from one leg to the other when they stand for a long time. Birds do the same thing to rest their legs, but pick one leg up entirely and tuck it under themselves.

Why don't the birds at the zoo fly out of the indoor exhibits that have no glass or bars to hold them in?

Sometimes birds do fly outside the exhibits, but they usually don't choose to do so. Everything they need for survival is inside: food and water; the right temperature; other birds; and light. Areas outside of their exhibits aren't very attractive to them because they are usually cool and dark and often noisy.

There are some bird exhibits at the zoo that were designed to allow the birds to fly freely about, while visitors walk on paths through their large exhibit areas. This is the case in several sections of JungleWorld and the World of Birds.

Reptiles and Amphibians

Were dinosaurs reptiles?

Dinosaurs were reptiles, and that's why looking at some of today's reptiles is like looking through a window into history. Although the word *dinosaur* means "terrible lizard," not all dinosaurs resembled lizards of today. In fact, it is more likely that they got their name because of their great size. Most modern lizards are tiny by comparison. Scientists believe that dinosaurs were not only bigger than today's reptiles, but also smarter and quicker.

Reptiles are **ectotherms.** This means that their body temperature changes when the air temperature around them changes. When reptiles sit on a rock in the sun, their body temperature rises. If they get too hot, they have to move to a shady spot—inside a cave or underneath a rock—to get cooler. Many reptiles are found in areas of the world where it is fairly warm year-round.

Those that live in cooler places have to hibernate in the winter. They go into a type of extended sleep in a warm place so that they won't die from the extreme cold. Human beings have a different heat-regulating system altogether. Unless we are sick, our normal body temperature remains 98.6° F, no matter how hot or cold it is outside. We cool ourselves off by sweating, which reptiles cannot do.

There are four kinds of reptiles: **crocodilians** (alligators and crocodiles), lizards, snakes, and turtles.

How are lizards different from snakes?
What do lizards eat? Do they lay eggs?

Lizards are four-legged reptiles, with five toes on each foot. Their bellies have many rows of scales, but snakes' bellies have only one row. Lizards have movable eyelids, whereas snakes have clear, protective scales covering their eyes, but no eyelids. Lizards have ear openings on the sides of their heads, and snakes have internal eardrums but no outer ears or ear openings.

The female lizard lays her eggs outside of her body (except in a few cases where the eggs hatch inside). She covers the eggs with sand, soil, dry leaves, or rocks, since she does not incubate, or sit on, the eggs. They hatch in one to three months, depending on the type of lizard, and the young can feed themselves right after birth.

Many lizards prey on insects. Plant-eating lizards find buds, leaves, or flowers by "tasting the air" with their tongues and **Jacobson's organ.** All reptiles have a Jacobson's organ, which is usually in the roof of the mouth. The Jacobson's organ is like a small computer that can analyze particles of air brought to it by the forked tongue and tell the reptile what is nearby, including food. Think about a sunny day in your house. When you look at the air coming in through a window, you can see millions of tiny dust particles floating around. Microscopic particles are always in the air, and these particles carry information which reptiles' Jacobson's organs can analyze.

Many lizards live in desertlike areas, and have developed special adaptations to survive in a climate of extreme temperatures and little rainfall. Lizards are most active either during cooler times of day, or at night. A lizard's urine is thick and not very watery, which helps them save liquid.

A collared lizard stands ready in its rocky habitat to catch a meal of insects or smaller lizards.

Some lizards have adaptations that help them escape when they are in danger. The fence lizard, for example, has a tail that will break off in a predator's mouth, allowing the lizard to escape. (The tail will eventually grow back.) The dab lizard, which has a very spiny tail, will escape predators by running into a hole in the ground, leaving its sharp tail sticking out. It can lash this tail back and forth to strike at predators outside the hole.

Do all lizards change colors, and how do they do it?

Some lizards (as well as some frogs) can change their colors, depending on their surroundings and their emotions. "Chromatophores," special cells in the lizards' skin, expand and contract to darken or lighten a lizard's color.

Where are turtles found?

Turtles, which look very much as their ancestors did 150 million years ago, are found all over the world, except in the polar regions. The main groups of turtles are the giant sea turtles, the land turtles and giant tortoises, and the freshwater turtles, or terrapins. All three groups of turtles have similar bodies, except for their size. The upper half of a turtle's shell is called the **carapace,** and the lower half is the **plastron.** This shell is both the turtle's protection and part of its skeleton. The backbone and ribs of a turtle are fused to the shell, making it impossible for a turtle to step out of its shell. The outside of the shell is made of thick scales, which are called **scutes.**

A bog turtle is well protected by its hard shell. On the left view is its carapace, and on the right is its plastron.

How old do turtles get and how big can they grow?

Many turtle species live one hundred years or more, but it's hard to tell a turtle's age simply from looking at its shell. Turtles vary in size from very small to very large. Giant tortoises, like the Galápagos and Aldabra species, can weigh over three hundred fifty pounds.

What do turtles eat?

Turtles do not have teeth. They use their sharp, curved, beak-like mouths to snap up food. The slider, a pond turtle, eats small animals, insects, and fish. The slider is a good swimmer, having a low, streamlined shell as all water turtles do. Its dark green coloring helps it to blend in with the dark, murky pond water, and makes it easier for it to sneak up on small prey. Other freshwater turtles may eat similar food.

Some land turtles are omnivorous, eating both small animals and insects as well as plants and berries. These turtles use their strong beaks to break off leaves and other plant material, and to also catch worms and bugs.

Some turtles are completely herbivorous, eating only plants. A few of the giant sea-dwelling species, like the green turtle, and most of the giant land tortoises are herbivorous. Some sea turtles, like the Atlantic ridley, eat a lot of jellyfish. In the oceans of today, plastic bags and jellyfish look very similar. Many ridley turtles die each year from eating plastic bags. In general, most sea turtles begin life eating plants (seaweed), and as they grow they begin to eat some animals as well, such as shrimp, squid, and jellyfish.

Do all turtles move slowly?

While it is true that many turtles are slow moving, sea turtles are capable of swimming rather quickly—some over 20 miles per hour. But most turtles do not need to move fast. Their bodies are usually as colorful as their surroundings—dark green in muddy water, speckled brown and yellow on forest floors—which helps to keep them camouflaged and able to sneak up on their prey. Some turtles have unique adaptations. The South American matamata looks like a pile of dead leaves on the bottom of the water. It even has leafy, loose skin around its head and body. When it senses a fish nearby, it stretches its neck out to grab the fish with its beak. The alligator snapping turtle has a wormlike piece of skin hanging in its mouth. This worm looks like food to an approaching fish. By the time the fish gets close enough to know that the worm is not real, the alligator snapper has a good chance of catching the fish for its own meal. And turtles, like all reptiles, use their Jacobson's organ to help them locate food. Even the giant sea turtles use this organ. They take large amounts of water into their mouths and remove particles to be analyzed before they push the water out again.

Turtles are also equipped with proper limbs for the habitat in which they live. Water turtles have webbing between their toes, sea turtles have flippers, and land turtles and tortoises have more solidly built legs for better walking. Turtles may not move quickly, but they are efficient.

How many eggs does the average turtle lay in one year?

All female turtles, including those that live in the oceans, climb onto the land at least once a year (sometimes two or three times) to lay eggs. The smaller land and pond turtles will lay no more than about a dozen eggs. The female uses the nails on her front feet to help dig a hole in the sand, soil, or pile of decaying leaves into which she deposits her eggs. The eggs will be incubated by the warmth of the material on top of them and by the heat of the sun. The sea turtle climbs onto the sandy beach, above the high-tide level of the water, and makes her "nest" in the sand using her flippers. This is a very difficult job for a turtle weighing as much as one hundred fifty pounds. She lays up to two hundred eggs at a time. The temperature in the nest determines the sex of the hatchlings: A cooler temperature of about 75 to 81° F will produce males; warmer temperatures of 88° F and higher will favor female hatchlings. Turtle hatchlings are an important source of food for many predators, and because of this fewer than half of the hatchlings survive to maturity.

What happens to turtles in the winter?

Turtles, like all other reptiles, need to take special steps to protect themselves in the winter. Pond turtles will dig underneath the mud at the bottom of a lake or stream. Land turtles dig under the soil or leaves on the forest floor or make burrows. There they hibernate until the warmer weather arrives. Large land tortoises do not need to hibernate since the temperature in their habitat is warm enough all year round. Sea turtles usually swim in warmer seas so they are not affected by winter weather.

How can you tell a male turtle from a female?

There are only a few visible differences between male and female turtles. Most females are larger than males. The tail of a male turtle may be much longer than a female's, and the plastron (lower shell) of the male is usually concave (curving upward), which helps during mating when the male mounts the female.

What is the difference between an alligator and a crocodile?

The snout (mouth and nose) of the alligator is rounder and shorter than that of the crocodile. Some of the crocodile's lower teeth do not fit into sockets in the upper jaw, so they stick out of the mouth and make the crocodile appear to be smiling!

Both crocodiles and alligators are known as crocodilians. Alligators are only found in two places in the world—America and China. The related caiman is from Central and South America. Crocodiles are found in Asia, Africa, Australia, and the Americas. The third type of crocodilians are the gharials from India, which are exhibited in the JungleWorld building. You can see Cuban crocodiles and Chinese alligators in the Reptile House, and caimans in the World of Darkness.

How are crocodilians born?

In the springtime, crocodilians make loud, deep sounds to attract mates. Later in the season, the female will build a nest for her eggs made of mud, branches, leaves, and grass. The female uses her snout to scoop these materials into a moundlike nest. An alligator or crocodile will deposit twenty or more eggs into the nest and then cover them up. The decaying of the nest materials will produce enough heat to keep the eggs warm and incubating for about two and a half months. During this time, the female, and sometimes the male, will stay near the nest to protect it from predators such as skunks and raccoons. Of all reptiles, crocodilians

Three broad-nosed caimans, recently hatched at the Bronx Zoo, all fit in the palm of a keeper's hand.

give their young the most parental care. When the young are ready to hatch, they will begin to make high-pitched sounds. The female helps to uncover the hatching eggs, making it easier for the babies to come out. The young are able to eat small animals like shrimp or crabs or insects as soon as they're born, but they must be protected from other, larger predators. When they are not looking for food, the babies can often be found during the day lying on top of the mother's head or back. American alligator babies stay with the mother for up to three years, while crocodiles stay for three to six months.

What do crocodilians eat?

A crocodilian's diet consists of fish, water birds, small aquatic mammals, and terrestrial mammals that might venture near the water. The sharp teeth of the crocodile are used to grab prey and tear it into pieces small enough to swallow.

Are all snakes dangerous to people?

Snakes are the most unusual looking of all the reptiles, and they are often the most misunderstood. Most of the snakes of the world are harmless to people. Those that are dangerous are found only in a few places around the globe. About one-seventh of the snake species in the United States are poisonous. On the other hand, most snake species are actually helpful to people because they rid their habitats of other animals considered pests, such as rats and mice. Farmers in the midwestern part of the United States are happy to share their fields with corn snakes for just that reason.

How do snakes catch their food since they can't run, and how do they swallow anything since their mouths are so small?

Snakes may not run after their prey, but their strong muscular bodies *can* move very quickly. The muscles found all along the snake's body push against the ground or tree on which the snake is moving. Sometimes snakes move in a straight line, the way an inchworm or caterpillar does, and sometimes they move in a semicircular or serpentine motion, going forward in large curves. Strong muscles also help snakes swim with ease.

The muscles that give snakes their locomotion also help them catch their food. Most snakes are called **constrictors** because of their means of obtaining food: They suffocate their prey by coiling their muscular bodies around it until it can no longer breathe.

To locate prey, a snake uses its special forked tongue to gather small particles of air to bring to the Jacobson's organ. Some snakes (like rattlesnakes and boa constrictors) also have heat-sensitive **pits** on their heads which help them to sense warm-blooded prey.

Poisonous snakes strike at their prey with their fangs. Fangs are special hollow teeth usually located in the front of the mouth. They are connected to glands in the snake's head in which poisonous saliva or venom is stored. When the snake bites its prey, the venom squirts into the prey animal's blood and attacks the nerves that control the heart and other muscles.

The rest of the snake's teeth also play a role. Since they are pointed backward in the mouth, when the snake begins to swallow they help push the prey deeper down the digestive tract.

After an Indian rock python hatches from its leathery egg, it is already prepared to find food and take care of itself.

A snake's mouth looks too small to actually swallow some of the animals it attacks. Here, too, snakes have special adaptations. Snakes have an elastic tissue, rather than a bone, connecting their upper and lower jaws, which can stretch a great deal. They also have an elastic tissue that allows them to expand their lower jaws from side to side while they eat. A snake can eat an animal one-and-a-half to two times bigger than the size of its head.

Why do snakes shed?

Shedding—replacing one set of skin with another—takes place more frequently when a reptile is growing a lot. When snakes are very young, they may shed as often as once every two months. Sometimes a snake will shed its skin if it has been hurt. As scar tissue grows around the wound, the snake may need to shed this damaged skin. Snakes continue to grow throughout their whole lives, but they do not grow or shed as much when they are older.

Even though it does not hurt the snake to shed, the time of shedding is a dangerous one. The dead skin has to come off all at once, including the clear scales covering the snake's eyes. When it's time for the snake to shed, these scales become cloudy and the snake is called "opaque." It can't see at this time and is in more danger of being harmed, so it may lash out at anything it thinks is threatening. An opaque snake may bury itself under sand or seek out a protected area until shedding is complete. Snakes use branches and rocks to help remove the old skin. They rub along the surface, peeling the old skin off inside out.

All reptiles shed their skins either in large pieces (snakes), smaller pieces (lizards), or one scale at a time (turtle scutes).

Why does the rattlesnake have a rattle?

Rattlesnakes are poisonous. When they are threatened by predators, they use their tail rattles to try to scare them. A rattlesnake would rather escape than fight, if it has a choice. The rattlesnake's rattle is formed at the end of the tail, where a hardened piece of dead skin is left each time the snake sheds. These loose pieces of skin make the rattling sound whenever the snake moves its tail.

At the Bronx Zoo, several species of rattlesnake are exhibited. These species come from many habitats, including deserts, grasslands, and riversides.

What is the difference between a reptile and an amphibian?

Amphibians date back over 280 million years, at least 50 million years before the first reptilian dinosaurs. Amphibians were the first animals to venture out of the water, though they never fully adapted to life on land. There are three separate orders of amphibians: frogs and toads, salamanders, and caecilians (legless, burrowing amphibians). Amphibians can be found all over the world, except where the earth is permanently frozen, or in deserts. Their skin is moist, and either smooth or warty, not scaly and dry like reptile skin. Amphibians lay clusters of jellylike eggs in the water, while reptiles lay dry, leathery eggs on land. Reptiles and amphibians are usually four-legged, but reptiles have claws on their toes, and amphibians do not.

Are all reptiles and amphibians slimy?

Actually, reptiles aren't slimy at all. Snakes may look especially wet, but that's because their skin is shiny. Amphibians, on the other hand, *are* slimy. They have mucous glands in their skin which produce a slimy substance that helps them breathe through their skin as well as their lungs.

What's the difference between frogs and toads?

It's not easy to tell the difference. A frog's skin is pretty smooth, while a toad's is rougher and looks warty. A frog's body is more streamlined than a toad's, probably because it spends more time swimming. Toads spend more time on land than frogs do. Even so, they do not jump as well as frogs and are larger and broader than frogs.

Why do frogs and toads make those loud sounds?

There are a couple of reasons for the sounds. Some frogs and toads will croak when there is a change in weather—as when tree frogs sing before a storm.

Sound is also the most important way for one frog or toad to attract another for mating. Some male frogs and toads have special sacs of skin around their throats that can be inflated while they are making sounds. The sounds then become much deeper and louder as the air vibrates over the vocal chords.

Almost all frogs and toads lay soft, moist eggs in the water. If a pond or lake is not available, a puddle on the ground or on a leaf will do.

How does a tadpole become a frog?

Young frogs and toads developing in eggs are called embryos. After several days inside a safe, jellylike egg, the embryo hatches. It is now a tadpole, breathing through gills like a fish, eating plants, and swimming through the water with the help of a long tail. As the tadpole grows, it starts breathing through inner gills. Its front and back legs begin to grow, and the tail disappears about a month after hatching. Soon lungs form, to help the froglet breathe on land. The froglet begins to eat insects and tiny water animals. The transformation, or **metamorphosis,** from jellylike egg to froglet is relatively short, but very complex!

How far can a frog jump? Is jumping the only way a frog can move around?

The distance a frog can jump is based on its size and the strength of its legs, which depend on what type of frog it is. Some bullfrogs can jump almost four feet, which is nine times their body size. Three-inch leopard frogs can jump five feet—twenty-one

The long, powerful legs of the small leopard frog aid it in swimming, and on land they enable the frog to leap as far as five feet.

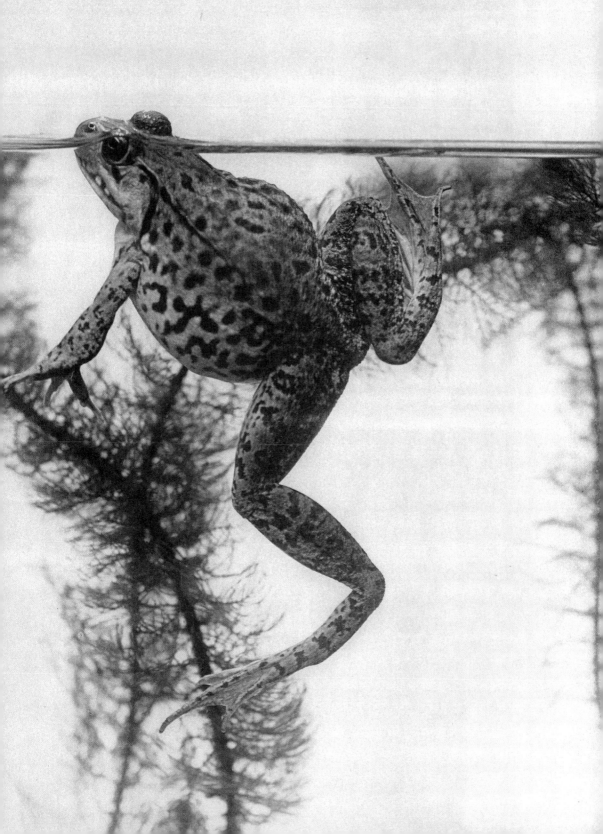

times their length. The African sharp-nosed frog (a tiny, two-inch frog) jumps an incredible sixty-five times its length.

Frogs don't only jump, however; they are also good swimmers, with long legs, webbed feet, and eyes positioned on top of their heads allowing them to stay underwater and yet see what's going on above the surface.

Tree frogs, which, as their name implies, live in trees, have a special adaptation for climbing on branches. At the ends of their fingers and toes are small disks which act like suction cups. Tree frogs also leap from tree to tree chasing insects. Their leaps are so graceful and acrobatic that they can catch an insect in midair before landing safely.

Are frogs and toads predators or prey?

Both! Frogs and toads are eaten by many animals, including birds like herons and egrets, mammals like wolverines and otters, reptiles like snakes, and even other amphibians, like the bullfrog. However, amphibians don't make very tasty meals, since most of them have the protection of some poison in their skin. A toad's skin tastes so awful that most animals will spit a toad out rather than eat it.

As predators themselves, frogs and toads catch and eat insects. When an insect is near enough, a frog quickly uncurls its sticky tongue to catch it. Some species of frogs and toads have no teeth, others have small ones used to grip their prey. In any case, frogs and toads don't use their teeth for chewing or tearing, just for holding and pushing food into the mouth.

Can you get a wart from touching a toad?

No. Although a toad's skin is bumpy and warty looking, a person cannot get a wart from touching it. Warts are thought to be caused by a virus.

Are salamanders related to lizards or frogs?

Like frogs, salamanders are amphibians, but they look a lot like lizards at first glance. A salamander's four legs are usually equal in length (a lizard's aren't), and the skin is smooth and moist like that of other amphibians. Salamanders do not have an outer ear; they "hear" by feeling vibrations through the ground and other solid objects. During the mating season, salamanders find each other by smell and touch rather than calls.

Aquatic Mammals

How do we know that whales are mammals, not fish?

Whales have hair (just a few, near their mouths), and nurse their newborn babies, called calves, with milk made by the mother. This makes them mammals. Mammals that spend most or all of the time in the water are called aquatic mammals; mammals that live in the oceans are referred to as marine mammals.

Since whales are mammals and not fish, they don't have gills, but breathe air as all mammals do. Their blowholes are on top of their heads, and work like nostrils. Through the blowhole a whale can take in enough oxygen to stay underwater for a long time, from fifteen minutes to an hour and a half. When whales exhale, the warm air from inside their bodies hits the cool outside air, forming water vapor called a "spout." It is called this because it looks as though the whale is blowing water through a spout.

Why are whales so big?

Whales actually vary greatly in size, from the fourteen-foot beluga to the hundred-foot blue whale. Scientists believe that millions of years ago the ancestors of whales lived on land. The hands they used on land evolved over time into pectoral fins, but hand bones can still be seen underneath the skin. The back legs disappeared, and flukes (tails) developed to help them swim. Whales have thick layers of blubber (fat) to keep them warm in cold water. Their bodies are streamlined, so that even though they are very large, they are still excellent swimmers.

How are toothed whales different from other whales?

There are two groups of whales, those with teeth and those with a tough membrane called baleen in their mouths. Toothed whales include beluga, killer, and sperm whales, as well as porpoises and dolphins. Killer whales can grow to thirty feet in length, and sperm whales to sixty feet.

Toothed whales are predators that hunt animals such as fish, squid, and octopus, and sometimes seals, dolphins, and other whales, too. Most toothed whales live in very large groups called pods. Sperm whales usually travel in a harem—one male with many females.

Baleen whales, which include sei, minke, humpback, fin, and blue whales, are very large but hunt the tiniest food. They eat small fish and **krill,** which is a type of crustacean related to shrimp. One whale must eat thousands of pounds of krill each day to survive. The baleen in the whale's mouth is called whalebone.

Beluga, *which means "white" in Russian, is the species name of this small, toothed whale from arctic waters.*

The edges of the baleen are fringed, which helps the whale to feed. The baleen hangs in "plates," each many feet long, covering the entire upper jaw of the whale. The whale opens its mouth, taking in large amounts of water and krill. Using its enormous tongue, the whale pushes the water out through the edges of the baleen, and the food remains in the mouth to be swallowed.

Do whales make any sounds?

Scientists have found that whales make lots of sounds. In one research project conducted by the New York Zoological Society, it was discovered that humpback baleen whales actually sing songs—a new one each year. The songs can be heard under the ocean for hundreds of miles. Whale songs are like bird songs in that the sounds are repeated in exactly the same order each time they are sung. If you listen to a tape of a whale song played at a fast speed, it sounds almost exactly like a bird song.

Toothed whales use sounds, too. They make clicking noises, and listen for echoes to tell them the size and location of objects ahead of them in the dark water. This is called **echolocation.** It is similar to radar or sonar and is the same navigating method used by bats.

What kind of animal is a seal?

Seals belong to a group of mammals called **pinnipeds,** which means "fin-footed." Pinnipeds include what are called "true" seals, eared seals, and walruses. There are eighteen species of true seals, including the harp, ribbon, leopard, gray, and elephant seal. True seals have no ears on the outside of their heads. Instead, they have ear holes that are opened and closed by muscles so that their ears do not fill up with water as they swim. True seals are better swimmers than walkers because they have to drag their back flippers when they're on land.

The other pinnipeds are the eared seals and the walruses. Sea lions and fur seals are eared seals. They have small external ears, but the openings underneath the ears close with muscles just like the ears of true seals. The eared seals' hind feet bend forward so they can walk on land with greater ease than true seals. Fur seals have an extra layer of soft fur on their bodies, which is one of the reasons they have been hunted and are now endangered.

All pinnipeds have many things in common: flippers, or fins (webbed skin with five toe bones underneath); streamlined bodies that help them adapt well to life in the water; a layer of blubber to keep them warm; sharp teeth for eating; and whiskers to help them locate food. They also all mate and give birth to young (called pups) on land. Pinniped mothers feed their young very rich milk.

In a replica of her California coastal habitat, a sea lion mother prepares to nurse her young pup.

This is important because the mothers must sometimes return to the sea to feed for a day or two, leaving the pups behind. Pups learn how to swim during the first month of life, but are often fearful at the beginning. Young seals learn how to hunt for fish at about four months of age.

Pinnipeds can dive to depths of from two hundred to a thousand feet, depending on the species. All pinnipeds can return to the surface quickly without getting dizzy. This is one reason why the U.S. Navy sometimes teaches sea lions to locate underwater objects and bring them up from great depths.

Pinnipeds vary a great deal in size. Harbor seals weigh 250 pounds, and gray seals 800 pounds. California sea lions are about 500 pounds, but stellar sea lions are 1,800 pounds. Fur seals can grow to seven feet in length and weigh 600 pounds, while elephant seals can grow to fifteen feet and weigh 5,000 pounds! Most male pinnipeds are much larger than the females.

The maximum age a wild seal lives to is about twenty years. Some are known to live as much as thirty-five years, and can usually live even longer in captivity. Although seals are predators, many animals hunt them, including killer whales, sharks, polar bears, and people.

Why does a walrus have tusks?

The walrus has the most distinctive appearance of all the pinnipeds because of its tusks. Tusks, which take over a year to grow, are used like rakes on the bottom of the ocean floor to find the clams and other shelled animals that walruses eat. The animal's beard whiskers scoop the clams off the sea floor. Walruses are very large; males can grow to eleven feet in length and three thousand pounds. Their skin is thick and tough, with only a little bit of hair. They are very good swimmers and divers.

Why do the sea lions at the Bronx Zoo make so much noise?

The noisiest sea lion at the zoo is the oldest male in the pool. His name is Bandit. Sea lions and other pinnipeds use their voices to communicate with each other. Bandit is telling every sea lion that can hear him that he is in charge of that pool and that group of females and pups. Making sounds is one way a male sea lion protects his harem or territory from being taken away by another male; if necessary, he'll also fight. Sea lion mothers and babies also use special sounds to find each other if they get separated. There are often sea lion pups at the Bronx Zoo, and you can hear their goatlike voices as they call to their mothers.

What kind of animals are otters, and how do they live in the wild?

Otters are found in water habitats on almost all continents. Their lifespan is from fifteen to twenty years. They spend most of their time swimming, but they also need the land. Their dens, which may have once belonged to other animals like rabbits, muskrats, or beavers, are usually underground, with an entrance underwater. This is where the female gives birth to up to five young. For five weeks, the helpless pups are protected in the den

A family of Asian small-clawed otters run and play among the mangrove tree roots and branches in JungleWorld.

and fed on rich mother's milk. The father does not share in family care until the young are about five months old.

Otters use scents to keep track of one another, and use sounds to communicate. They use a coughlike alarm call when there is danger, and a scream to signal anger. When they are in a playful mood they chirp, and they use this chirping sound both above and below the water.

River otters are part of the weasel family, which also includes ferrets, skunks, minks, and sea otters. River otters spend most of their time in and around fresh water. They have a slender, flexible body, with short legs, webbed toes, and a strong tail—all adaptations for efficient swimming. Their small, round ears close when they go underwater, and so do the nostrils on their broad noses. They have long whiskers which help them catch prey (fish, crayfish, amphibians), and sharp teeth to help them eat. In the winter, North American river otters hunt underneath the ice for long periods of time without surfacing for air. This is because they're able to find air pockets underneath the ice.

You can see the Bronx Zoo's river otters in an outdoor exhibit near the Reptile House. In the JungleWorld building, there is a family of small-clawed otters from Malaysia—which have been successfully breeding in captivity.

Are otters as playful as they look?

Otters often chase and slide around playfully. In addition to having fun by doing this, they are also practicing ways to move quickly in the event of danger. When otters travel on land, they run much better than they walk. On mud or snow, they slide on their bellies to get places fast. Otters use their legs for running on land, for steering in water, and for stopping.

What's the difference between a river otter and a sea otter?

The major differences are the kind of water they live in and their size. Sea otters are found in salty oceans rather than fresh water where river otters live, and weigh up to eighty pounds (four times the size of river otters). One exception is the giant otter, a river otter living in South America, which can grow to six feet and weigh seventy pounds.

Sea otters rarely leave the water, and are well adapted for an aquatic life. They clean their baggy fur by rolling over in the waves to get rid of scraps of food and other dirt, and by grooming themselves with their claws. Having clean fur is very important because otters do not have a layer of blubber underneath their skin, and must stay warm and keep afloat by trapping warm air underneath their fur. If the fur is dirty, this becomes difficult.

Sea otters dive as deep as one hundred feet for food, using their large, webbed hind feet to push them down to the sea floor. There they find food such as mussels, abalone, and sea urchins. They float on their backs when they're on the surface of the water, and use rocks as tools to break open the shells of mussels and other food. Then they eat as they float along.

Otters live in large beds of seaweed called kelp. Groups of otters are called rafts. Females and pups live in rafts by themselves, and males live in other rafts. Pups are born in the water and can swim only a little bit at birth. The mother holds her pup on her belly, or leaves it holding on to kelp while she swims to find food. It takes about a year for a mother to teach her pup how to swim and hunt well enough to survive on its own in the rough ocean.

Does a sea cow give milk?

Sea cows should not be confused with dairy cows. Sea cows are called cows because they graze the way cows do, but they graze on marine plants, algae, and seaweed, not on grass. The sea cow family includes the manatees from Florida and South America, and the dugongs from Africa, Malaysia, and Australia. Seen from a distance, sea cows look half human and half fish. In fact, they probably gave rise to the legend of mermaids.

Sea cows have small heads and bottle-shaped bodies, and grow from eight to fourteen feet long. They prefer shallow water, even though their paddle-shaped tails make them good swimmers. Manatees and dugongs usually live in small herds or family groups, and are harmless, gentle creatures. Calves are born in the water and stay with their parents for about two years.

Just like elephants, who also graze, manatees and dugongs have molar teeth that constantly wear out and are replaced by new ones. The upper lip overhangs the lower one and is covered with bristly whiskers that help to pull out plants to eat. A sea cow's lungs are very large, enabling it to hold its breath and feed under-water for fifteen minutes at a time. The nostrils are located on top of the snout and close when the animal is underwater. Sea cows have poor eyesight but make up for it with excellent hearing, sense of smell, and sense of touch.

Many sea cows are threatened with extinction today. Manatees are suffering because the plants they feed on grow in waterways that people use for boating. Sometimes people pull out these plants to make it easier for boat travel, and this makes it difficult for the animals to find food. Another serious problem is that boat propellers wound and kill the manatees. In some places, sea cows are hunted for their skin, flesh, and teeth. But they are now pro-tected from hunters in the United States and some other countries where they live. It is hoped that the research being done in Florida and Brazil will help these species to survive.

Nocturnal Animals

Why do some animals stay awake at night?

Nocturnal animals are those that are active during the night hours and sleep in the daytime. Because of this schedule, they avoid competing for food with diurnal animals—those which are active during the daytime. This is especially important for animals that hunt for their food, such as black leopards. Being nocturnal helps prey animals like mice and wood rats as well, since it enables them to avoid daytime predators (even though they still have to protect themselves at night). Many desert animals are nocturnal, avoiding the extreme heat of the desert days.

Are nocturnal animals different from other animals?

Many of the senses of nocturnal animals are specialized and well-developed for night living. If you've ever awakened in the middle of the night and tried to find your way around, you know how important the sense of touch is in the dark. Some animals have whiskers to help them feel their way in the dark, or to locate food.

It takes people's eyes a long time to adjust to the dark. Nocturnal animals' eyes are different; they can adjust to low light quickly. In the **retina,** the light-sensitive part of the eye, every nerve fiber ends in either a very tiny cone or a very tiny rod. The cones give us sharp vision and help us to see colors; the rods allow us to absorb light. Chemicals found in the rods and cones, along with vitamin A, help the eye to adjust to either bright or dim light. Nocturnal animals' eyes have more rods than diurnal animals do, and pupils (the black part in the center of the eye) that can open very widely to take in all available light. Some pupils also contract to a slit shape, which shields the rods from bright light. The rods are also protected by a special membrane called the tapetum—a layer of green, mirrorlike cells located behind the retina. Light is reflected off the tapetum instead of being absorbed by the eye. You can see the tapetum working if you shine a light at a nocturnal animal. Its eyes will appear sparkly because the tapetum is working to increase the response of the light-sensitive cells. Since a good supply of vitamin A is necessary for better eyesight, many nocturnal hunters instinctively eat their prey's liver first, because vitamin A is stored in the liver.

Nocturnal animals also have a well-developed sense of hearing—much, much better than humans. Some nocturnal animals, like funnel-eared bats and Australian bandicoots, have large or unusually shaped ears to help bring sound directly to the ear. The fennec fox of Africa has such large ears that it can hear a mouse breathing in the dark night. An owl's two ears are each shaped differently, and may be higher on one side of the head than the

With its large ears and excellent sense of hearing, a fennec fox can detect its prey in the dark desert night.

other. The position of the ears enables the owl to locate prey very precisely by gathering sounds at different levels. Caimans (alligators from South America) communicate with sound, and their ears are protected from the water by movable flaps of skin and muscle.

The sense of smell is also important to nocturnal animals. A predator, such as the wolf, must locate its prey by scent. And a prey animal, such as a rabbit, must be able to smell an approaching predator if it is to have a chance to escape. Even omnivores, like the opossum and the skunk, rely on their keen sense of smell to locate food. **Megabats,** which are fruit- and flower-eating bats from the tropical regions of the **Old World,** find most of their food—overripe bananas, guavas, figs—with their noses. You can tell if an animal has a good sense of smell by observing the size of its snout (nose). The larger the snout, the better the sense of smell.

Does the expression "blind as a bat" have any truth to it?

Although most bats do not depend on their eyesight for flying or finding food, they certainly can see and are not at all blind. Nectar- and pollen-eating bats find food with their noses *and* their eyes. The flowers they eat are often light-colored, which helps the bats find them.

Do bats get tangled up in people's hair?

In spite of the stories some people tell, it would be very unlikely for a bat to accidentally get caught in a person's hair, since bats have a way of detecting exactly what's in their path, and will almost always try to avoid contact with humans if they can. **Microbats,** found in most areas of the world, navigate by a system called echolocation: The bat makes high-pitched sounds, and then waits for an echo to tell it if any objects are in its path, as well as the shape and size of those objects. When an insect-eating bat is hunting, it begins searching for its food by sending out about ten pulses (sounds) per second. As it approaches possible food sources, it increases the pulses to fifty per second. Finally, in what is called the terminal phase of the hunt, two hundred echolocating pulses are sent out per second. Using this method, a bat can not only locate something as small as a moth, but can even pick out the species of moth it prefers to eat. Bats are the only mammals that can fly, and they fly almost as well as birds do.

Do bats always hang upside down?

Yes. A bat's leg bones are very thin, so thin that the animal can't support its own body weight when standing. Having thin legs helps to keep bats lightweight, however, which is good for flying. When resting, bats spend most of their time hanging upside down in caves or lying flat in rock crevices. They can hang by both of their hind feet, or only one, and are able to clean themselves while hanging by using their free hind foot. Vampire bats, which eat blood, walk around much more than other species of bats. This is necessary because they eat a great amount at one time, over-filling their stomachs and making it difficult for them to fly.

What do bats eat?

There are over nine hundred species of bats; most of them eat either insects or fruit. Many species will be mentioned here by their Latin names (in italics) because most bats are not known

Fruit bats, like the Rodriguez in the World of Darkness, hang from tree branches by day and fly off at night in search of food.

by common names. *Noctilio* is a fish-eating bat. Its fur is greasy to protect the animal from wetness. Noctilio uses echolocation to find fish in the water. Grabbing a fish with its claws, this bat can stuff chewed fish into its cheek pouches, storing the food to digest later so that it can continue hunting.

Insect-eating bats, like *Myotis lucifugus* (little brown bats), can eat one-third of their body weight in insects in about one and a half hours. This species is very common in the United States. Tropical species can eat as many as twelve hundred fruit flies in an hour, scooping the insects up with their wings and bringing them to their mouths.

Fruit-eating bats like the Indian flying fox eat while hanging upside down from a branch, using one wing to bring fruit to their mouths. The juices are sucked from the fruit, and most of the pulp and seeds fall to the forest floor. This process is important to rain-forest ecology because the bat helps spread seeds from the fruits it eats, helping new fruit trees to grow. This is called **seed dispersal.**

Many fruit-eating bats are also pollen eaters. Pollen is the powdery substance that's spread from plant to plant for repro-duction. While feeding on flowers, bats often get pollen on their hair, some of which they ingest and the rest of which is later dropped onto other flowers when the bat lands on them and grooms. Fruit-eating bats get extra protein in their diets from eating pollen, and also from eating the insect larvae (eggs) often found in overripe fruit.

Some species, such as *Megaderma lyra,* eat rodents, birds, frogs, and other bats. Other species eat only blood. The three blood-drinking species live in Central and South America. They are called vampire bats, and they have a very good sense of smell. *Desmodis,* one of these species, uses its sharp incisor teeth to make a small cut in the skin of a sleeping animal, like a cow. The bat uses its tongue and saliva to keep the blood flowing. Although one cut would not harm a cow, sometimes many vampire bats feed on the same animal, or come back night after night. This can cause serious blood loss for the animal, and even death. In places where vampire bats live in large numbers, people often try to keep bats away so that they will not endanger herds of domestic animals or bother sleeping people. Many species of bats often live together in one cave, so scientists are trying to find ways to remove vampire bats without accidentally harming the other, helpful species.

How are bats born? How does a mother bat find her baby in a cave where there are large numbers of hanging bats?

Females hang upside down when they give birth. They use one wing to form a pouch to catch the infant bat as it is born so it doesn't fall to the ground. Gestation is two to eight months long, depending upon the species. Most mother bats can recognize the scents of their babies, as well as their sounds. They also remember where they left the babies hanging. In some species, such as the Mexican free-tailed bat and the long-fingered bat, a mother may nurse any baby she finds, but in most species a mother finds her own young. Often, the baby bat will hold on to the mother's fur and be carried on feeding trips. *Myotis* females leave several "baby-sitters" behind to watch the young while they go out hunting.

Megabats, which are large Old World bats, live in colonies, but each family within the colony lives in its own home. At the Bronx Zoo, Old World Indian fruit bats can be seen in the JungleWorld building. In the World of Darkness are flying foxes, lesser long-tongued bats, and lesser spear-nosed bats.

At what age does a bat learn to fly?
How long do bats live?

Bats begin flying when they are fully grown in size, at about two to four months of age. They do not reach adulthood, or have their adult fur, until they are about two years old. Bats live between five and twenty years. It is impossible to tell the exact age of an adult bat.

Do bats migrate as birds do?

Most bats live in warm parts of the world and do not migrate. Those that live in cooler climates hibernate rather than migrate, because hibernation requires less fat to be stored in the body. When bats hibernate, they look for a cave or other area with high humidity and a low, stable temperature above freezing (above 32° F). As the temperature gets colder and colder outside, the bats move farther into the cave. Once a bat has established where it will hibernate, its body fat is turned into energy very slowly, enabling the bat to live off its fat for a long time.

Can you see nocturnal animals at the Bronx Zoo?

Yes. In the World of Darkness building at the zoo, most of the lights are kept off in the exhibits during the day, so that the animals think that it's nighttime and stay awake. This gives visitors the chance to see nocturnal animals in an active state. The lights that are used in the exhibits are colored and don't bother the animals, since they can't see colors very well. For example, in the bush baby exhibit, the tree limbs on which these small primates leap are lit with a combination of blue and white light. The tree that the bush babies sleep and rest in, however, is lit with red light. Similarly, in the desert exhibit, the snake and rodent burrows are lit with red to set them apart from the rest of the habitat, which houses cacomistles (relatives of the raccoon).

In the World of Darkness, the exhibits are kept dark from 10 A.M. to 10 P.M. From 10 P.M. until the following morning, bright lights are turned on in the building to imitate daytime. In this way, by reversing day and night, the zoo allows the animals the proper amount of time needed for both activity and rest.

The galago, a primitive nocturnal monkey from Africa, has large eyes and ears to help it find its way around dark treetops.

Primates

What is a primate?

Primates are considered to be the most advanced of all the mammals. They generally have large, well-developed brains, are warm-blooded, have flexible hands and feet, and fur or hair covering some or all of their bodies. Humans are just one of the 203 species in the primate order.

There are four kinds of primates: prosimians or premonkeys, Old World and **New World** monkeys, apes, and human beings. One simple way to tell monkeys from apes is that most monkeys have tails, and apes do not. There are some exceptions, however: The Barbary Ape of northern Africa—which, despite its name, is a monkey—is almost tailless. Also, monkeys are usually smaller than apes.

Where do primates live?

With the exception of human beings, who inhabit just about every part of the world, primates mostly live in the warm, tropical regions of Central and South America, Africa, and southern Asia. A few primates do live in cool regions, though; the thick-furred macaque monkey of Japan, which can withstand cold and even snow, is one such primate.

Why do monkeys live in trees?

Trees provide monkeys with three important things—a ready supply of food, a place to rest, and safety from predators. Monkeys and other primates have special adaptations that help them climb vines and trees and live an arboreal existence. Most important, they have five separate fingerlike digits on each of their hands and feet, including an opposable thumb. (If you touch your thumb to the other fingers on your hand, you can understand how having such a thumb can help primates grasp and hold things with just one hand.) All primates, except people, have big toes that are opposable, too, so they can use their feet as well as their hands to climb.

Most primates have flat fingernails rather than claws, which make it easier for them to move through trees. Marmoset monkeys and some of the prosimians, however, do have claws or clawlike nails.

Almost all primates spend at least some of the time in trees, even if they are not actually tree dwellers. Because of their large body size, some apes, like the gorillas and chimpanzees of Africa,

The smallest of all the apes, the white-handed gibbon spends most of its time in trees, often leaping as far as thirty feet from branch to branch.

spend most of their time on the ground, though their young climb trees, and the whole troop will sometimes sleep in trees at night. When they're on the ground, gorillas and chimps have an unusual way of walking—they walk flat-footed on their hind limbs, but on the knuckles of their forelimbs.

The other two types of apes—the orangutans and gibbons of Asia—spend most of their time in trees. Gibbons are the most agile and acrobatic of all the apes—swinging easily from branch to branch using a special hand-over-hand movement called brachiation. At the Bronx Zoo, we have both white-handed and white-cheeked gibbons.

Human beings, of course, live completely on the ground, but still have a lot in common with the tree dwellers. We have hands that can grasp tightly, keen eyesight (with binocular vision), and good coordination. Vision is very important to arboreal animals because they must be able to jump through the branches of tall trees without falling, and find and hold onto food (such as fruit and leaves) while balancing in the trees. They must be able to see things both close up and far away.

Most primates rely on their sight even more than their sense of smell, and that's why they generally have shorter noses and larger eyes than other mammals. Prosimians, however, which are not as advanced, have a better sense of smell than other primates. Prosimians are nocturnal, whereas humans, monkeys, and apes are generally diurnal, with some exceptions. And the howler monkeys of South America are **crepuscular**—active at dawn and dusk.

Do monkeys have color vision?

Yes. Their color vision helps them to find food in the trees, and to distinguish ripe fruit from unripe fruit. Also, some monkeys have brightly colored faces and bodies, which play a role in finding and attracting mates.

Nocturnal primates do not have color vision.

Do all monkeys hang upside down? If so, why?

Monkeys generally do not hang upside down for long periods of time, like bats. But some, like the spider monkeys of South America and Mexico, can hold on with only their tails and hang upside down for short periods of time. They look like big spiders when they hang by their tails, and that's how they got their name. Tails that can be wrapped around branches and used as an extra hand or foot are called prehensile tails. Most monkeys and pre-monkeys have tails, which is important in helping them keep their balance up in trees, but not all tails are prehensile.

New World monkeys live in Mexico, and Central and South America, and include spider, howler, squirrel, and woolly monkeys, as well as marmosets, tamarins, capuchins, titis, sakis, uakaris, and douroucoulis (the only nocturnal New World monkey). A few have prehensile tails, including the capuchin, howler, spider, woolly, and woolly spider monkeys.

Old World monkeys, from Asia and Africa, do not have prehensile tails, so it's not surprising that they spend less time in trees. Macaques, of Asia, have short tails and are on the ground for much of the day traveling in bands led by experienced male leaders. Patas monkeys live in troops on the African savannah, feeding on the ground while one male stays on guard in a tree keeping an eye out for danger. Baboon troops mostly stay on the ground, but sleep in trees or on cliff ledges at night. Baboons live in closely knit social groups whose female members keep peace among the troops. Other Old World monkeys include langurs (which look like spider monkeys), colobus monkeys, guenons, mangabeys, mandrills, and geladas.

There are other differences between Old and New World

monkeys, too. New World monkeys have bare, flat faces, large **craniums,** small eyes, thick fur, small thumbs, and separated nostrils. Some species have claws. They are said to be a quieter, gentler group of animals than Old World monkeys.

Old World monkeys have nostrils that are close together and pointed downward, well-developed thumbs, and big, bare, colorful patches on their backsides called ischial callosities.

Why are some monkeys called "premonkeys"?

About 75 million years ago, when dinosaurs were dying out, the first primates came into being. These primates were tiny, insect-eating, molelike creatures, and they ranged all over the world. Their descendants are today's premonkeys. Premonkeys are less advanced than monkeys, falling somewhere between leaf eaters (like lizards) and monkeys (that eat leaves, insects, and fruit). The scientific name for a premonkey is a prosimian. Because prosimians are very ancient primates, scientists study them to learn about human ancestry.

Today there are only a few remaining species of prosimians. They live in the tropical regions of the Old World—in Africa and Asia—and are mainly nocturnal. Prosimians generally have large eyes, a good sense of smell, longer arms than legs, claws, and pointed muzzles (snouts) covered with hair. Because of their poor temperature-regulating systems, some of them go into a state of inactivity during the dry season and in cool weather.

The prosimians include the lemurs of Madagascar (an island off the coast of Africa), which are endangered due to the loss of their forest habitats; the diurnal sifakas, indris, and avahis; the lorises of Africa and southern Asia; the tarsiers from the Philippines, Borneo, and Sumatra; and the aye-ayes.

What is a bush baby?

Bush babies, also called night apes or galagos, are African prosimians with long bushy tails, thick fur, and long rear legs that help them leap great distances. They are nocturnal, coming out at night to search for insects, eggs, and fruit. One unusual characteristic of bush babies is their ability to fold their ears down when frightened. The name bush baby comes from the babylike cries these animals make.

At the Bronx Zoo, bush babies can be seen in the World of Darkness, a building that is kept dark during the day so that visitors can see nocturnal animals awake and active.

Why do small orange monkeys live together with large gray ones in JungleWorld?

Both of these animals are silvered leaf monkeys, a type of langur from the lowland rain forests of southern Asia. Babies of this species are born with orange fur, which turns to gray when they are about five months old. It's believed that the bright color helps adult monkeys find them easily, and also acts as a warning to adults to be careful when handling them. Young babies are passed around the entire troop right from birth, a rare practice among monkeys. Mothers allow other adults, probably relatives, to "baby-sit" when they are busy looking for food.

Silvered leaf monkeys roam in troops led by an adult male. The male wakes the troop in the morning with a loud call, and the day is begun in search of food—leaves, buds, flowers, and insects. If one troop of silvered leafs meets up with another, the dominant males will confront and chase each other to determine which will stay in that territory. Should a dangerous predator, say a leopard, come near a troop, the dominant male monkey will bark loudly and leap about, giving the other monkeys a chance to climb nearby trees to safety.

Which are the monkeys with the really big noses?

These are called proboscis monkeys, and they were given that name because *proboscis* means long snout or nose. It is the males that have the large noses, which they use to give loud warning honks to their troop when a predator is close, or to make loud snorts to end disputes between youngsters. It is believed that only mature, dominant males have these large noses.

One of the male proboscis monkeys at the Bronx Zoo is named Ed. He was wounded in the wild, and arrangements were made with the Malaysian government in Asia for Ed to come to the Bronx Zoo, where he became a part of the zoo's troop. At first, fresh mangrove leaves had to be shipped in each week because that was the only food Ed would eat, but soon he developed a taste for other, more readily available leaves.

For all leaf-eating monkeys at the zoo, keepers cut and clip mulberry and other leaves from around the zoo, and store the extras in freezers. Some monkeys are also fed green beans, yams, eggs, rice, peanut-butter sandwiches(!), and commercial primate chow.

Proboscis monkeys are a social species that live in the mangrove forests of Borneo, which is in tropical Asia. The mangrove trees they inhabit grow along bays where salty ocean and fresh waters mix. The trees help stabilize the land by keeping the waters from washing away the soil, and also provide food for many different animal species.

Troops of proboscis monkeys usually consist of a male, several females, and youngsters. In the wild, troop sizes range from six to sixty individuals, with females often moving from one troop to another. At night several troops may gather together.

As an adult female and a juvenile look on, an adult male proboscis monkey (right) keeps a lookout for danger.

Proboscis mothers are very attentive to their infants, allowing other troop members to play with the baby only under supervision. Newborns have bluish complexions and gray hair.

Proboscis monkeys are an endangered species, and the Bronx Zoo has the first troop of breeding proboscis in the United States.

What is a baboon's favorite food?
How much does it eat?

Baboons are omnivorous, eating everything from insects and eggs to fruit, grains, roots, and buds. When they go out foraging together they can eat enormous quantities of insects and other food. Baboons live in the rocky regions of Africa and Arabia, and are not tree dwellers. Baboon troops are often very large, containing up to three hundred individuals.

How do primates communicate?

Primates communicate with each other in a variety of ways. First, they "talk" to each other, using barks, shrieks, squeaks, hoots, honks, whistles, or grunts. Gibbons, for instance, are loud hooters. Hooting is a type of communication that works well in the leafy forests because they can't easily see each other through the dense foliage. Hooting serves to call families together, keep unwelcome visitors away, and mark territories.

Primates also communicate through body gestures such as changes in posture and facial expressions. When there is danger they may wave their arms and jump about to warn others. Staring, yawning, and showing canine teeth may all be used as threat gestures and dominance displays.

For some monkeys, like the Geoffrey's tamarin of Panama and Costa Rica, the sense of smell plays a key role in communication. These monkeys use **secretions** from special scent glands on their bodies to mark their territories.

Monkeys also spend a lot of time grooming each other. By combing their fingers through each other's fur they remove dead skin, loose fur, and parasites, which helps keep them clean. But more than that, grooming and touching helps family members to **bond,** or feel close to one another, which is very important to social animals. Monkeys live in both small and large groups. Some, like the squirrel monkeys of Central and South America, live in groups with as many as five hundred members.

As with other primates, verbal and nonverbal language (touch, gestures, expressions) are essential means of communication among humans, helping us maintain complex relationships and social bonds. Some apes—gorillas and chimpanzees—have been successfully taught to communicate with people using American Sign Language, and have learned to use several hundred signs.

What are the smallest and largest primates?

The smallest primate is a monkey called a pygmy marmoset which lives in the tropical forests of Peru, Ecuador, and Columbia. It weighs only 3½ to 4⅕ ounces, and lives on a diet of tree sap, fruit, and flowers.

The largest primate is the gorilla of Africa. Male gorillas can weigh up to four hundred pounds.

Are gorillas dangerous? What kind do you have at the Bronx Zoo?

Though they are big and extremely strong, gorillas are peaceful animals. They will not fight unless they are cornered and need to defend themselves or their families.

Gorillas are vegetarians, and do not kill to eat. Adults eat up to fifty pounds of food—stems, leaves, fruit, roots, bamboo shoots, and insect eggs—a day. They move slowly, spending most of their time feeding.

Gorillas live in stable family groups of up to thirty or forty individuals. A mature, dominant male, called the "silverback," lives with his females and young. A large group can sometimes have more than one silverback, but only one will be dominant. The leadership of a mature, experienced male is important to the safety of the group. Among other things, an older male can recognize traps and keep his group away.

Silverbacks lead their groups on daily searches for food. At midday, during their rest period, youngsters play, some gorillas groom (gorillas are very clean animals), adults sleep, and silverbacks keep peace within the group. In the afternoon, the group feeds again. At night, the gorillas make nests of leaves to sleep on. Their nests are only used once, since gorillas never sleep in the same nest twice.

In nature there are about thirty-five to forty thousand lowland gorillas. There is another kind of gorilla, too—the mountain gorilla. Only about four to six hundred of these gorillas are left in the wild. Both the lowland and mountain gorillas are endangered. The gorillas we have at the Bronx Zoo are lowland gorillas.

How big are baby gorillas when they're born?
Who cares for them?

At birth, baby lowland gorillas weigh only about four and a half pounds. Adult males can grow up to four hundred pounds; females are smaller. Females are mature at about age eight or nine, and can have up to six babies in their lifetime (one about every four years). To attract mates, male gorillas will perform courtship displays and roar to show how strong they are. The

The silverback gorilla has an important job—protecting the family group as it spends its day searching for food and resting.

females choose the strongest gorillas to mate with so their babies will have the best chance of survival. The gestation period is about nine months.

All baby gorillas at the Bronx Zoo are raised when they are very young by women called surrogate mothers rather than their real gorilla mothers, because sometimes the gorillas aren't experienced enough to raise their own babies properly. Also, gorillas raised by surrogate mothers can be more easily treated by the zoo's veterinarians should they become ill. Gorillas are a highly endangered species, and the zoo works hard to be certain that each baby survives. Later, when they are older, they live together with other gorillas.

What are the similarities and differences among orangutans, chimpanzees, and the other apes—especially in their habitats, intelligence, and behavior?

Orangutans are arboreal apes that live in the forests of Borneo and Sumatra, in Southeast Asia. They are much larger than gibbons, and move through the trees more slowly. On the ground they walk awkwardly because their legs are short and weak. Orangutans are about two-thirds the size of gorillas, and have longer arms than both gorillas and chimpanzees. They are covered with long reddish-brown hair that can grow to be a foot long. Orangutans eat mostly fruit and buds. Like gorillas they build nests of leaves and branches to sleep on at night, but continue to use the same nests for several evenings. Unlike gorillas, orangutan males do not live with their families. Adult males live apart from the females except during mating. Maturity is reached in this species at age ten. A full-grown orangutan weighs about one hundred sixty pounds and is four-and-a-half feet tall. Mother orangutans give birth to only one offspring at a time, which they nurse for one and a half years. As in all primate species, the mother is very loving toward her baby, protecting it from harm, feeding it, and teaching it how to do things. Orangutans learn at almost the same rate as chimpanzees. The gorilla is considered about equal in intelligence to the orangutan, but does not have the great curiosity of the chimp.

The chimpanzee is an **anthropoid ape** that lives in the forests of equatorial Africa, and is smaller and more arboreal than the gorilla. Chimpanzees have highly developed brains, and anatomies similar to people. It has recently been found that humans and chimps are 99-percent genetically similar. Chimpanzees are extremely curious, have excellent memories, and are capable of great affection (which they express through touch, pats, hand-holding, and embraces). Like gorillas, chimpanzees have been participants in programs designed to teach them American Sign Language; some have learned to recognize up to 350 signs, and use one hundred fifty correctly. The chimpanzee's intelligence is considered greater than that of all other primates except humans.

Chimpanzees live in either family units of a mother and some of her young, or all-male bands that travel and feed together. Bands of chimpanzees may belong to larger groups of up to eighty individuals, which forage together for vegetables and fruits during the day. At night they sleep in trees in the nests they build. Chimps reach maturity at seven or eight, and can live up to fifty years of age. Mothers bear one young, after a gestation period of eight to nine months.

Endangered Species

What is an endangered species?

An endangered species is one that is in danger of becoming extinct. When an animal's population has decreased to such a small number that the species may not be able to survive, it is considered endangered. And when the last member of a species has died, that animal has become extinct—it no longer exists. An effort to protect animals or plants from becoming extinct, or to protect the environment, is called conservation.

Endangered species can be found all over the world. Some species were never very plentiful to begin with; they are considered "rare," but not endangered. Animals whose populations are on the decline and may become endangered if nothing is done to help them are called "threatened."

Animals that no longer have any place to live in the wild are considered "extinct in nature." Zoos may be the only hope for these animals' survival. One such animal, the Mongolian wild horse of Asia (also called Przewalski's horse), became extinct in nature in the 1950s after years of being heavily hunted for its meat. Small herds of these beautiful yellowish-brown horses live at the Bronx Zoo and at other zoos around the world.

The Mongolian, or Przewalski's, wild horse, the only true wild horse in existence, came very close to extinction from hunting.

Is it natural for animals to become extinct?

As long as there has been life on earth, life forms have been dying out. Many species of dinosaurs once roamed the earth, and later became extinct. This is a natural process. In recent years, though, the rate of extinction has increased drastically. Scientists say that in the early days of life on this planet only one animal species may have become extinct every thousand years. Today, that rate is more than one per *day*.

Every species of animal and plant plays an important role in nature; every time a species vanishes, the natural world doesn't work as well as it used to. Because all life forms are connected, creating an **ecological balance,** nature will be harmed if we lose too many species and that balance is disturbed.

The screen outside JungleWorld at the zoo shows the number of acres of jungle that are being destroyed every minute. Who is tearing it down?

The jungles are being torn down by people. Just two hundred years ago, there were fewer than a billion people on earth; thirty-five years ago there were less than 3 billion people; and today there are more than 5 billion. As the population grows, more and more resources are needed to feed and house people. Land is cleared to farm crops, raise animals for food, build homes and roads, and for lumbering (selling wood to be used for such things as furniture, paper products, and cooking fuel).

When forests are cut down or burned, the animals and plants living in them lose their homes—and they usually can't find new ones. Habitat destruction is the biggest single threat to survival that animals face today, and it is human activity that causes it. In an animal's habitat, there is food, shelter, and safe places to raise young. So to save animals, habitats must be protected.

Are jungles and rain forests the only lands being destroyed?

No, they're not. But the loss of jungles and **rain forests** in South America, Central America, Africa, and Asia has been devastating to many animals. Between fifty and a hundred acres of tropical rain forest are torn down every minute of every day! And considering that one-half to three-quarters of all plant and animal species on earth are sheltered in the rain forests, this is a very serious problem.

When rain forests are taken down, often to clear large areas for farming, animals lose their homes. And what makes this even sadder is that the farmers don't end up with very good farmland, anyway. Rain forest soil is of very poor quality for farming: Most of the nutrients are stored in the lush plants and trees, rather than in the earth, because the heavy rainfalls wash them away.

Another type of habitat that is being destroyed is wetlands, such as swamps and marshes. They are drained and filled in for housing projects and other developments. Wetlands are important in nature because they absorb and store rain water, prevent flooding, and provide homes for aquatic wildlife.

In North America, as our cities have grown, large stretches of grassland, prairie, marshes, swamps, fields, and forests that may have existed for many, many years have been eliminated. Every

Yong-Yong, a giant panda, visited the zoo in 1987. Very few pandas are alive today due to large-scale habitat destruction in China.

time we erect a power plant, a dam, or a housing development, we displace animals that once made that site their home. Every time oil is spilled, or we dump poisonous waste into the ocean, we disrupt nature, and threaten all other life forms.

Why does the giant panda like bamboo so much? What is making it endangered? Where do pandas live?

Most of the surviving thousand or so pandas in the world live in small, protected reserves in China; about 100 pandas live in zoos, but are not breeding well. Pandas once ranged throughout most of eastern China, in elevations of six to fourteen thousand feet, and they now live in tiny pockets of their former range.

As the Chinese people have moved farther and farther into the pandas' territory, much of the pandas' habitat has been destroyed, making it harder and harder for the animals to survive. Because of this, as well as the fact that many types of bamboo—the main part of the pandas' diet—died out during the 1970s and 1980s, many pandas have died of starvation despite efforts by the Chinese government and conservation organizations to save them. A panda must eat large quantities of bamboo every day because it is not very nutritious and the panda's system is not well adapted for digesting it. When an animal is dependent mostly on one food source and habitat destruction makes that food hard to find, that species will most likely become endangered. And that is what happened to the panda.

Other factors have contributed to the giant panda's problems. Before the Chinese government passed laws to protect them, pandas were hunted heavily and taken as specimens for zoos. Also, pandas can only give birth once every year, to one baby (born weighing only about five ounces), which then stays with its mother for one and a half years of parental care. When it takes a long time for an animal to reproduce itself, as it does for the panda, that animal is said to have a "low reproductive rate." And when a species cannot breed quickly, its chances of becoming extinct increase. No pandas live at the Bronx Zoo today, but two (Ling-Ling and Yong-Yong) came for a six-month visit in 1987.

Are snow leopards considered an endangered species?

Yes. Snow leopards became endangered as a result of being hunted for their fur. Hunting an animal for fashion items or jewelry is called "market hunting." Most of the other big cats of the world are also endangered, including cheetahs, jaguars, leopards, Asian lions, ocelots, and Florida panthers.

Hunting has taken its toll on many reptile and bird species,

A successful breeding program for snow leopards is helping to save these beautiful endangered cats from extinction.

too. Large sea turtles, for instance, are declining rapidly in number all over the world, hunted for their meat, eggs, and beautiful shells. When animals are hunted in large numbers for food, it is called "commercial hunting."

Hunting has been responsible for the endangerment of many animal species, especially since the invention of the gun. In 1800, a handsome bird called the passenger pigeon, with shiny blue plumage and a chestnut-colored breast, numbered in the billions in North America. By the early 1900s, it was extinct as a result of uncontrolled hunting.

Snow leopards were first exhibited at the Bronx Zoo in 1902. In 1966, the first litter was born at the zoo. Since then, sixty-two snow leopard cubs have been born as a result of the zoo's highly successful captive-breeding program.

Did buffaloes become endangered because of hunting?

The American bison, also called the buffalo, once numbered over 60 million on North America's western plains; it was saved from extinction when its population dropped to fewer than one thousand because of sport hunting.

Though American Indians had hunted bison for centuries, this did not cause the animal's downfall. The Indians took only the animals they needed, and used every part of the body—the hide for clothes, moccasins, wigwams, and canoes; the bones for tools and weapons; and the meat for food. Hunting for survival is called "subsistence hunting," and doesn't usually cause endangerment. And since the Indian populations were small, the number of bison killed was not that great. But when the railroads were built out west, great numbers of settlers from the East went to the plains and slaughtered massive numbers of bison primarily for sport.

One of the earliest conservation efforts of the New York Zoological Society was to help save the North American bison, which was almost extinct by the end of the nineteenth century. The first director of the newly formed society, William T. Hornaday, founded the American Bison Society and raised the money to preserve the few remaining bison, which were moved to protected reserves and provided with food and shelter. By 1905, the bison population had increased to over sixteen hundred, and today the animal is no longer in danger of extinction. A captive-breeding program was also successfully undertaken at the Bronx Zoo, and a herd of bison lives at the zoo today.

Why are whales hunted?

Land animals are not the only ones to be hunted. Many species of whales, seals, and otters have become endangered because of hunting. Until the 1900s, whaling was one of America's largest industries (whales were hunted for meat, oil made from their blubber, and tools made from their teeth and bones), but as the animals' numbers grew smaller and smaller, citizens of the United States pressured the government to ban whaling. The United States and other countries formed the International Whaling Commission in 1949, but not all the countries that signed agreed to eliminate whaling altogether, and several countries did not participate. In 1972, the United States Congress passed the Marine Mammal Protection Act, which prohibits killing of, or trade in, products made from marine mammals. This act has helped dolphins and other marine mammals as well as whales, but more protection is needed worldwide.

What's the biggest danger to eagles, especially the bald eagle?

Eagles are predatory birds—hunters. Some, like the golden eagle and the imperial eagle, eat mammals. Others consume mostly fish, aquatic birds, and some carrion.

The fish-eating bald eagle of North America, the national symbol of the United States, is an endangered species. Three things made the bald eagle endangered—being hunted, loss of its own hunting areas, and exposure to a certain kind of pollution. In the 1940s, widespread use of a pesticide called DDT was begun in the United States to kill insects that were destroying food crops. It was not known for a long time that DDT sprayed on the soil was washing into lakes, oceans, and rivers, and poisoning the creatures living there. The chemical was absorbed into the fish living in the waters, and then into birds like the bald eagle, brown pelican, osprey, and peregrine falcon, which ate the fish. Most of the time the birds survived, but when the females laid their eggs, the shells were so thin and fragile that they'd crack when the adult birds sat on them to incubate them. The babies inside the eggs would then die.

Pesticides and other toxic chemical pollutants can destroy whole communities of animals; this is another form of habitat destruction, just as serious and deadly as the tearing down of an animal's habitat.

127

Though DDT has been banned in this country (it's still used in other countries), to this day its effects still show up in aquatic birds. Other environmental pollutants have taken their toll on dolphins, beluga whales, and other marine mammals. Oil spills in the oceans have also been catastrophic for many aquatic birds. Once waters are polluted, they may never become completely clean again.

Land mammals have suffered from other forms of chemical poisoning. The North American black-footed ferret is very close to extinction because of poisoning. As farmers in the West converted vast prairies into farms and cattle ranches, they tried to rid themselves of prairie dogs—small rodents that live in underground burrows. Prairie dogs are seen as competitors for grass and crops, and their tunnel networks are a danger to livestock, which can fall in the holes. Widescale poisoning was begun, and the result was that not only were large numbers of prairie dogs killed off, but the black-footed ferret, which preys on prairie dogs, died out, too. Today only a handful of these ferrets are left alive, and the New York Zoological Society and others are working to save them. Prairie dogs have not become endangered because, unlike ferrets, they reproduce quickly and can choose from a number of readily available food sources.

Is it true that elephants are hunted just for their tusks?

Yes. Large numbers of elephants have been killed by hunters simply for their ivory tusks. Most of this hunting is done illegally, and is referred to as "poaching." The elephant's tusks are a special kind of very long front incisor teeth. Despite laws to protect them, many elephants lose their lives just because of the greed of hunters. In the 1930s, there were 10 million African elephants alive; today there are only 650,000, and their numbers are decreasing rapidly.

Black rhinoceroses are extremely endangered today because of a similar situation. Rhinos are killed by hunters for their horns. Some people in Asia falsely believe that ground-up rhino horns have magical powers, and they spend a lot of money to obtain them.

Millions of snakes and crocodiles have also been victims of this kind of hunting. Their skins have been turned into purses, belts, and shoes. And a bird called the scarlet ibis, of South America, has been killed for its beautiful feathers.

Another cause of species endangerment is the exotic pet trade. When people make pets out of wild animals, especially endangered ones, they remove them from their natural homes and reduce their numbers in nature. Many exotic animals for sale in pet stores have been captured from the wild and brought into this country illegally. Parrots are often smuggled into the United States, and many die along the way. Even such ordinary animals as box turtles can suffer from being removed from the wild. Many people don't know what to feed a turtle, or how much warmth it requires. Often, the turtle dies.

Another danger to wildlife comes about when settlers and travelers bring animals to a place where they are not native. This is called "exotic introduction." In the Hawaiian Islands, pigs, goats, cats, and rats were introduced, and the result was the extinction of several native bird species.

The Indian rhinoceros and her baby shown here will not have to face the dangers of poaching and loss of habitat that they would in the wild.

Do you think it is helpful to save endangered animals and keep them in zoos? What are some endangered species at the Bronx Zoo?

There are over 950 known species of endangered and threatened animals and plants in the world. Each year, more are added to the Endangered Species List.

There are five major reasons to save species. The first reason is to maintain the earth's ecological balance. Second, studying animals and nature is the best way to learn about life. Third is the moral issue—that animals have just as much of a right to live as human beings do. Fourth, many medicines have been discovered from studying plants and animals. If we do lose species, we may decrease our chances of finding cures for diseases. And last, every time we lose an animal or plant species, some of the beauty and uniqueness of nature is lost forever.

If we are to save endangered species, we must provide them with secure habitats until there are safe places once more in nature for them. This is where zoos play a key role.

The Bronx Zoo shelters and breeds many endangered and threatened species. Among them are: gelada baboons, Siberian tigers, Asian elephants, gibbons, lowland gorillas, snow leopards, cheetahs, proboscis monkeys, Grévy's zebras, South American condors, white-naped cranes, parrots, Chinese alligators, and Cuban crocodiles. Signs in front of the exhibits indicate which animals are endangered.

What other efforts does the zoo make to help endangered animals?

The Bronx Zoo is taking many different steps to help endangered species. The zoo's conservation division, called Wildlife Conservation International (WCI), studies endangered animals in many countries and helps determine how to save them and their habitats. WCI researchers work closely with governments and scientists in Africa, Asia, and Latin America, to plan long-term conservation projects. These plans may include the creation of game reserves or national parks, the enforcement of laws to protect endangered species, the training of local zoologists and researchers, and the education of local people about the value of saving wildlife and preserving the environment. In an emergency situation—when a species is in immediate danger of extinction—WCI may step in and offer direct help. Currently, the zoo is working on a project to help save the highly endangered black rhinoceros of East Africa.

Ongoing field projects include studies of clouded leopards in Thailand, crocodiles in Venezuela, proboscis monkeys in Borneo, lowland gorillas and elephants in Africa, and gazelles and other large mammals in Tibet.

At the zoo, captive-animal management goes on daily, and endangered species are bred under the captive-breeding program. Additionally, the Education Department teaches school children and adults about endangered species.

Have any endangered species bred only in captivity been successfully returned to the wild?

Yes. Two good examples are the peregrine falcon and the bison. By the late 1970s, the peregrine falcon population in the United States had dwindled down to only about six hundred. As the result of an intensive conservation effort, three thousand captive-bred peregrine falcons have been released in recent years to wilderness areas, increasing their numbers substantially. Peregrines have also been released in various cities across the United States, including Denver, Los Angeles, Chicago, Boston, Albany, Philadelphia, Minneapolis, and Milwaukee.

The American bison, or buffalo, came close to extinction in the late 1800s. Its population dropped from 60 million to fewer than one thousand. Due to efforts mainly on the part of the New York Zoological Society, the bison was saved. Today there are between 20,000 and 30,000 bison living in refuges and parks throughout the country.

The New York Zoological Society has been involved in species conservation work for over ninety years. The society maintains the

Wildlife Survival Center on St. Catherine's Island off the coast of Georgia. Some of the world's rarest and most endangered species are bred there.

What laws protect endangered species?
What do you think the future is for them?

Organizations throughout the world are working to help save wildlife. In 1972, the Marine Mammal Protection Act was passed by the United States legislature, and in 1973 the Endangered Species Act was passed. The Endangered Species Act is an important law because it protects all threatened native wildlife (mammals, birds, reptiles, fish, insects, plants, etc.) in the United States.

The United States has also banned the import of some endangered animals used in the pet and fashion trade, but greedy people sometimes break the laws.

The laws that have been passed are steps in the right direction to help protect endangered animals. But laws are only meaningful if they are strict and if they are followed—and people have to understand the problems affecting our environment and the reasons to save life forms if they are to respect the laws that are passed. The future for endangered species is in everyone's hands.

One of the worldwide organizations that supports scientific study of endangered species issues is the International Union for the Conservation of Nature and Natural Resources (IUCN). IUCN's Species Survival Commission keeps a record of every endangered or threatened species. IUCN started the Convention of International Trade in Endangered Species (CITES) in the 1970s. The organization, which has been joined by more than ninety countries, arranges for international agreements and treaties on animal protection.

In 1981, the Species Survival Plan was devised by the American Association of Zoological Parks and Aquariums (AAZPA) to preserve wild animals. Through this plan, zoos in North America and other countries work together to strengthen captive populations of endangered species.

How can I help protect wildlife?

There are many things you can do to help. First, learn as much about endangered species and about nature as you can by reading books and articles and watching nature shows on television. Teach others what you learn, and encourage them to participate, too.

For house pets, keep only animals that have long been domesticated—dogs, cats, and some birds, such as parakeets. These animals make the best pets, and can often be found through local humane societies and shelters. Do not try to make pets out of animals that were captured in the wild.

When you go on nature walks, don't pick up plants or animals. You can enjoy seeing animals and taking photographs of them without disturbing them. Sometimes baby animals may seem to be lost, but usually they are not. Their mothers are often close by, but will not come out of hiding until you're gone. So leave the wildlife in the wild.

Recycling can also make a big difference to the environment. The products you use every day—paper, glass, cans, clothes—are made from materials taken from nature. The more you reuse and conserve these things, the less resources have to be taken from nature to replace them.

Many communities have recycling centers. Encourage your family to participate. When you recycle, you produce less trash, and less trash means less pollution. Avoid purchasing products packaged in Styrofoam and nondegradable plastics; these wrappings can take many, many years to decompose into the earth. Use cloth napkins instead of paper; paper bags instead of plastic; reusable cups; refillable pens; and so on. If you live outside the city, you might want to start a compost heap in your backyard, to recycle vegetable and plant wastes into healthy fertilizer for your garden.

Don't buy products made from wild animals, such as boots or belts made out of snake, elephant, or crocodile skin; jewelry or carvings made of illegally obtained ivory; coats or hats made of the fur or feathers of endangered animals. When everyone stops buying these products, no one will find it profitable to trap and kill animals, and the fur and exotic pet trades will end.

Writing letters to government officials to get stricter laws passed to help endangered animals is of great value. You can write to your mayor, representatives, senators, and even the president of the United States to tell them that you think more and stronger laws should be passed to save endangered species, and that existing laws should be better enforced. Find out what these officials are doing to help, and what more can be done.

Finally, support zoos that are breeding endangered animals, and conservation organizations that are helping to preserve them in the wild. If your family is interested in joining the Bronx Zoo, you can write to: New York Zoological Society, Bronx Zoo, Membership Department, Bronx, New York 10460.

Did You Know?

Do hummingbirds hum?

Hummingbirds beat their wings so rapidly that a humming sound is produced. That's how they got their name. The reason they need to beat their wings so fast is so they can hover in front of flowers or feeders while inserting their bills inside to draw out nectar and insects.

There are over three hundred species of hummingbird, and they range all over the Americas and in the Andes. The smallest bird in the world is the bee hummingbird, which is only two-and-a-quarter inches long. Hummingbirds can fly upward, downward, sideways, and backward.

What is the tallest animal in the zoo?

The giraffe can grow to eleven feet at the shoulder (seventeen to nineteen feet at the crown), and is not only the zoo's tallest animal, but the tallest terrestrial mammal in the world. Though the giraffe's neck is so long, it has the same number of vertebrae (bones) in it as humans do (seven), though the giraffe's are obviously much longer. Having such a long neck is helpful for spotting enemies at a distance, and also for feeding on high tree foliage.

There are only two animals in the giraffe family—giraffes and okapis—both of which are from Africa. The giraffe family is a branch of the deer family. Okapis are brown with white stripes on their legs. They grow to six-and-a-half feet tall, and have such long tongues that they can clean their eyes with them.

What is a Tasmanian devil?

A Tasmanian devil is a small marsupial mammal living in Australia. It moves slowly, has strong jaws that can crush bones, and feeds on carrion, poultry, and snakes.

What are the longest snakes at the zoo?

The anaconda and the Indian python are the zoo's largest snakes—measuring over twenty feet long—and they are two of the largest snakes in the world. Both snakes are constrictors. The anaconda is native to swampy areas in South America, where it spends much of its time in the water looking for prey—birds and

It took six keepers at the New York Zoological Society's Annual Meeting to measure this twenty-foot reticulated python from India.

mammals. It can also climb trees and bushes. In the wild, anacondas have been reported to reach lengths of thirty feet. The Indian python lives in mangrove swamps, scrub jungles, and rain forests in Southeast Asia, India, and Indonesia. In the daytime, this snake sunbathes or rests in a cave or other safe place. At night, it comes out to hunt for birds, mice, small deer, and civets. When the female of the species lays her eggs (up to one hundred of them), she wraps her coils around them and incubates them for sixty to eighty days, moving them slightly to keep them in sun or shade. Once born, the young are on their own.

What is the fastest animal at the zoo?
What is the slowest?

Cheetahs are the zoo's fastest animals. They can run at speeds of up to sixty-nine miles per hour—but only for short spurts. They run to chase their prey, which include birds, hares, jackals, small antelope, and ostriches. Cheetahs are from Africa and Asia, and measure from three and a half to four and a half feet, with twenty-five- to thirty-inch tails.

Perhaps the slowest-moving animal at the zoo is the Hoffman's two-toed sloth, a South American mammal that spends almost its whole life upside down on the branches of rain-forest trees. Sloths eat the leaves, buds, and flowers of tropical plants. Though they are not primates, you can find them at the Bronx Zoo in the Monkey House.

Where are poisonous spiders found?

Almost all spiders have venom glands, but in most cases the amount of venom they can inject is very small—only enough to kill small prey. A few spiders have venom strong enough to disable or even kill a human. The chief among these is the black widow spider (*Latrodectus*), which lives in warm climates all over the world, including North America. It uses a type of venom called a neurotoxin that causes paralysis and severe muscle cramps. Other dangerous spiders live in South America (*Phoneutria* and *Loxoscides*), Australia (Sidney funnel-web spider), and South Africa (Button spider). (The Latin names are used here because these spiders do not have common names.) Not all spider venom is neurotoxic. Some cause serious ulcerations, or sores, on the skin. The tarantula does not bite with enough venom to seriously harm or kill a person, unless the person is allergic to insect stings.

Which animals can stay underwater longest?

Sea lions and most seals can stay underwater for twenty minutes, while the Weddell seal, which dives more than eighteen hundred feet to find food, can stay submerged for almost an hour.

Sperm whales, which descend more than three thousand feet in the water, can stay below for over an hour. Their heartbeat slows down, and they have an efficient means of storing and transporting oxygen in their body.

Some turtle species can stay under for extremely long periods of time. Turtles normally do not use as much oxygen when they breathe as mammals do, and they don't need to take as many breaths. When sea turtles go down to the sea floor to sleep, they have an adaptation that allows them to take oxygen out of the water and absorb it into their bodies through special skin sacs. This allows them to stay underwater for up to three hours. In oxygen-rich water, slider and loggerhead turtles can stay down even longer.

Can some animals change their own fur colors?

The snowshoe hare, which lives in Alaska, Canada, and the northern part of the United States, has a dark brown coat in the summer that turns white in winter to help camouflage it in the snow.

Hares are close relatives of rabbits. Rabbits and hares are not rodents, though they are often mistaken for such. They are lago-morphs, which also include the pika family. There are seventy different species of rabbits and hares living all over the world. They are herbivorous mammals whose long hind limbs enable them to run fast. They have long ears, small tails, and teeth adapted for gnawing on vegetation. Pikas look a lot like rabbits, but are smaller in size and have shorter ears. They live in mountainous regions in Asia, and in the Rocky Mountains in North America. During the day, pikas gather up large amounts of plant matter, which they then dry and store among the rocks.

What's the largest animal in the Bronx Zoo?

The elephant is not only the Bronx Zoo's largest animal, but is the biggest terrestrial mammal in the world. Asian elephants can measure up to eighteen- to twenty-one-feet long (including the trunk), and weigh five to six tons. African elephants can weigh over thirteen thousand pounds (six and a half tons) and measure as long as twenty-four feet (trunk included). The zoo's Asian elephants can be seen at the center of the zoo, in the newly renovated Elephant House.

Glossary

adaptation   A characteristic of a species that developed over a long period of time to help that species survive in its habitat. Examples: a seal's flippers, a camel's hump.

altricial   Young animals that are completely dependent on their parents for some time after birth are altricial. Examples: eaglets, gorillas.

amphibians   Animals that begin life in water, and later live both in water and on land. Examples: frogs, toads, salamanders.

anthropoid apes   The four primates thought to be closest to humans: gibbons, orangutans, gorillas, and chimpanzees.

aquatic   Living on, in, or at the edge of the water. Examples: mallard ducks, otters.

arboreal   Living in trees. Examples: monkeys, squirrels.

binocular vision   The ability to focus on an object with both eyes at the same time. Examples: owls, humans.

bond   A close relationship between two or more animals. Bonds form between mothers and young, and among members of a group of social animals. Examples: a mother sea lion and her pup; the females in a troop of baboons.

bower An arched passageway of grass and twigs built by male bowerbirds to attract females.

brachiation The special ability of some animals, especially gibbons, to swing from branch to branch by stretching one arm over the other.

breeding The mating of male and female animals, which produces young.

brood A group of young animals belonging to one set of parents, or the activities of parents in caring for their young. Example: A mother duck warming her ducklings with her wings.

browse Twigs, shoots, and leaves of plants.

camouflage The coloration of an animal or species that protects it in its habitat. Examples: a tiger's stripes, a parrot's colorful feathers.

captive bred Describes animals that are born in zoos, parks, and so on, and not in the wild.

captive propagation Long-term zoo and conservation breeding projects designed to help save species that may one day be returned to the wild.

carapace The upper shell of a turtle or tortoise.

carnivorous Eating only the flesh of other animals. Examples: lions, bald eagles.

carotenoids Substances found in animals, such as crustaceans, and plants, such as carrots, that, when eaten, aid in maintaining the coloration of some birds' feathers.

carrion The flesh of dead animals, which is eaten by scavengers.

clutch   A group of eggs laid by one female.

conservation   Actions to help save an animal, an area of land, or other natural resources.

constrictor   A snake that kills its prey by suffocating it.

cranium   The skull of an animal, or the bones that enclose the brain.

crepuscular   Active during twilight hours—at dawn or dusk. Examples: rabbits, deer.

crocodilians   Crocodiles, alligators, caimans, and gharials.

crop   In birds, the area at the bottom of the esophagus where undigested food is stored.

crustacean   A spineless animal that has jointed legs and is covered by a hard outer "skeleton." Examples: shrimps, crabs.

deciduous   A tree that loses its leaves seasonally, as opposed to an evergreen tree.

den   A protected place where young are born and raised, or a place where an animal hibernates.

depth perception   The ability to judge the distance of objects. Animals with good binocular vision, such as monkeys, usually have good depth perception.

digits   The name given to fingers and toes.

diurnal   Active during the daylight hours. Examples: flamingos, zebras.

dormant   In a sleeplike, inactive state.

echolocation   A system of navigating and locating objects by bouncing sounds off objects.

ecological balance   The natural condition or state of relationships among the plants, animals, and other organisms in a habitat.

ectotherm   An animal whose body temperature changes in relation to sources of heat outside the body. Reptiles and amphibians are ectotherms.

embryo   The prebirth or prehatching stage of an animal.

endangered species   An animal found in such small numbers that it is threatened by extinction and may not survive.

endotherm   An animal with an internal means of generating and regulating its body temperature. Mammals and birds are endotherms.

esophagus   The gullet, or tube, through which food passes on its way to the stomach.

extinct   When the last member of a species has died, that species is extinct. If an animal lives only in zoos or preserves, but not in nature, that animal is extinct in the wild.

forage   To search for food, usually of the plant variety.

gestation   The period of time in which a mammal develops inside its mother's body before birth.

gizzard   In birds, the muscular area in front of the intestines in which food is ground down.

gland   An organ in the body that produces a necessary fluid.

habitat   The specific type of area an animal lives in. Examples: wetland, desert.

herbivorous   Eating only plants. Examples: giraffes, prairie dogs.

hibernate To go into a state of sleep for a long period of time (usually the winter). All body functions, such as heartbeat and respiration, are slowed down to conserve energy.

hydroponic Plants grown in nutrient-rich water rather than soil. At the Bronx Zoo, hydroponic grass is grown to feed many of the herbivores and omnivores.

incubate To keep eggs warm until they hatch, usually by either sitting on them or covering them with vegetation or sand.

invertebrate An animal without a backbone (spine). Examples: insects, spiders.

Jacobson's organ In snakes and some lizards, a sensing organ in the roof of the mouth that detects and interprets scents from particles in the air picked up by the animal's forked tongue.

keel The middle part of a bird's breastbone that is attached to the strong flight muscles.

keratin The substance that forms hair, feathers, the outer layer of skin, fingernails, horns, hooves, and scales.

krill A tiny crustacean eaten by baleen whales.

larva The youngest stage of insect life.

locomotion The way in which an animal moves. Examples: walking, swimming.

marsupial A mammal without a placenta, whose young develop in a pouch rather than a uterus. Examples: kangaroos, opossums.

megabats Old World, fruit-eating bats.

metamorphosis A process of change in an animal's structure occurring after birth. Example: tadpoles transforming into frogs.

microbats   Insect-eating bats of both the New and Old Worlds.

midwife   Someone (human or animal) who helps a female animal during the birth process.

migration   A seasonal move by an animal or species, usually preceded by a change in weather conditions or a decrease in available food.

molt   In birds, to shed feathers periodically so they can be replaced by new ones.

monocular vision   The ability to focus on an object with only one eye at a time. Examples: pigeons, hummingbirds.

New World   Name given to the western hemisphere: North and South America.

nocturnal   Active during the dark, night hours. Examples: bats, raccoons.

Old World   Name given to the eastern hemisphere: Europe, Asia, and Africa.

omnivorous   Eating both plants and animals. Examples: people, brown bears.

opposable   A thumb or other digit that can touch the other fingers or digits of the same hand, giving the ability to manipulate small objects.

oviparous   Producing eggs that develop outside the mother's body.

pectoral   Referring to something on the chest area of an animal. Example: pectoral fins on a whale's chest.

pinniped   Fin-footed animals: seals, sea lions, walruses.

pits   In snakes, openings near the lips that detect heat from other sources.

placental   A mammal that develops before birth inside its mother's uterus.

plastron   The lower part of a turtle's or tortoise's shell.

precocial   Young animals that are active and independent after birth. Examples: snakes, turtles.

predator   An animal that hunts and eats other animals. Examples: lions, ferrets.

preen   In birds, to clean and straighten the feathers with the bill.

prehensile   Referring to something that can grasp or hold, like the tails of some monkeys or the trunk of an elephant.

prey   An animal that is hunted and eaten by other animals. Examples: Thompson's gazelles, chickens.

primates   Humans, apes, monkeys, and premonkeys.

rain forest   A habitat containing tall evergreen trees where the temperature constantly stays around 80° F and the annual rainfall is between eighty and two hundred inches.

retina   The light-sensitive layer of the eye that receives images from the lens and creates vision.

rodent   A gnawing animal with two pairs of incisor teeth (upper and lower jaw) that grow continuously. Examples: mice, squirrels, cavies.

savannah   An open plain or grassland in a tropical climate.

scutes   In reptiles, especially turtles, bony or horny plates, or large scales.

secretion   In animals, a fluid released from a gland.

seed dispersal   The spreading of plant and tree seeds by animals. Usually seeds are accidentally dropped during eating, or when an animal eliminates.

shed   In reptiles, when the outer layer of skin peels off to make room for a new layer of skin. In invertebrates, like lobsters and tarantulas, the entire outer shell, called the exoskeleton, is shed.

species   A related group of animals that are able to breed and produce healthy young.

tarn   A small mountain lake.

terrestrial   Living on the land. Examples: elephants, ostriches.

territory   A specific area in a habitat within which an animal feeds, mates, and protects itself from intruders.

ungulate   A four-legged, hoofed mammal. Examples: pigs, horses.

venom   A substance secreted from a poisonous snake's mouth when it bites its prey which affects the nervous system and helps the snake to catch the prey animal.

vertebrae   The bones of the spinal column.

veterinarian   A medical doctor who specializes in the treatment of animals.

wean   To get a young mammal used to eating foods other than its mother's milk.

Bibliography

Allen, Martha Dickson. *Meet the Monkeys*. Englewood Cliffs, N.J.: Prentice-Hall, 1979.

Bell, Joseph. *Official Guide to the Bronx Zoo*. New York: The New York Zoological Society, 1980.

Berger, Gotthart. *Monkeys and Apes*. New York: Arco, 1985.

Big Cats Zoobook. San Diego: Wildlife Education Ltd., 1987.

Bridges, William. *A Gathering of Animals*. New York: Morrow, 1974.

Browne, Thomas, ed. *The Animal Kingdom: The Mind Alive Encyclopedia*. Secaucus, N.J.: Chartwell Books, 1977.

Burn, David M., ed. *The Complete Encyclopedia of the Animal World*. London: Octopus Books, 1980.

Burton, Maurice, ed. *The New Larousse Encyclopedia of Animals*. New York: Bonanza, 1981.

Campbell, Bruce, and Elizabeth Lack. *A Dictionary of Birds*. Vermillion, S.D.: Buteo Books, 1985.

Cochran, Doris M. *Living Amphibians of the World*. Garden City, N.Y.: Doubleday, 1972.

Cook, David, and Valerie Pitt. *A Closer Look at the Big Cats*. New York: Franklin Watts, 1975.

Dixson, A. F. *The Natural History of the Gorilla*. New York: Columbia University Press, 1981.

Grzimek Animal Life Encyclopedia, Volume 10. New York: Van Nostrand Reinhold, 1972.

Hill, John E., and James D. Smith. *Bats: A Natural History.* Austin, Tex.: University of Texas Press, 1986.

Huntington, Harriet E. *Let's Look at Reptiles.* Garden City, N.Y.: Doubleday, 1973.

Lambert, David. *Reptiles.* New York: Gloucester Press, 1983.

Macdonald, David, ed. *Encyclopedia of Mammals.* New York: Facts on File, 1985.

McFarland, David, ed. *The Oxford Companion to Animal Behavior.* New York: Oxford University Press, 1987.

Mohr, Charles E. *The World of Bats.* New York: Lippincott, 1976.

Moyle, Donald, ed. *The Life of Reptiles and Amphibians.* Morristown, N.J.: Silver Burdett, 1978.

New York Zoological Society. *New York Zoological Society Annual Report.* 1986–87.

Peterson, Roger Tory, and the editors of Time-Life Books. *The Birds.* New York: Time-Life Books, 1968.

Pope, Clifford H. *Snakes Alive and How They Live.* New York: Viking, 1965.

Rüppell, Georg. *Bird Flight.* New York: Van Nostrand Reinhold, 1975.

Scott, Sir Peter, ed. *The Amazing World of Animals.* New York: Praeger, 1976.

Shreeve, James. *Nature: The Other Earthlings.* New York: Macmillan, 1987.

Silverberg, Robert. *The Auk, the Dodo, and the Oryx.* New York: Thomas Y. Crowell, 1967.

Taglianti, Augusto Vigna. *The World of Mammals.* Maidenhead, Berkshire, England: Sampson Low Guides, 1979.

Wallace, George J., and Harold D. Mehan. *An Introduction to Ornithology.* 3d ed. New York: Macmillan, 1975.

Whitfield, Philip, ed. *Macmillan Illustrated Animal Encyclopedia.* New York: Macmillan, 1984.

Yalden, D. W., and P. A. Morris. *The Lives of Bats.* New York: Quadrangle, 1975.

Index